Mandala Quilt Designs

Katie Pasquini

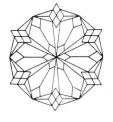

Dover Publications, Inc.
New York

Typesetting by Artcraft Printers, Eureka, California.
Diagrams and illustrations by Katie and Chris Pasquini.
Photos by Lindsay W. Olsen.
Editing by Randi Loft and Kathleen McCombs.

Published in Canada by General Publishing Company, Ltd., 30 Lesmill Road, Don Mills, Toronto, Ontario.
Published in the United Kingdom by Constable and Company, Ltd., 3 The Lanchesters, 162–164 Fulham Palace Road, London W6 9ER.

Bibliographical Note

This Dover edition, first published in 1995, is a republication of *Mandala*, originally published by C & T Publishing, Lafayette, California, in 1983.

Library of Congress Cataloging-in-Publication Data

Pasquini-Masopust, Katie.
     [Mandala]
     Mandala quilt designs / Katie Pasquini.
          p.   cm — (Dover needlework series)
     Originally published under title: Mandala. Lafayette, Calif. : C & T Pub., 1983.
     Includes bibliographical references.
     ISBN 0-486-28491-3 (pbk.)
     1. Patchwork—Patterns. 2. Quilting—Patterns. 3. Quilts. 4. Mandala.
I. Title. II. Series.
TT835.P367   1995
746.46—dc20   94-40103
                                                                       CIP

Manufactured in the United States of America
Dover Publications, Inc., 31 East 2nd Street, Mineola, N.Y. 11501

To Mom

There are many people I would like to thank for making this book possible.

Chris Pasquini for his wonderful drawings, encouragement and faith, for without him there would be no book, a very special thank you.

Tom and Mark Pasquini for their support;

And the rest of the family: Larry, Totsie, Meg, Austa and Ed, for being there.

Randi, Michael, and Aaron for letting me on all the rides free at Perklo Park.

Lindsay Olsen for being so patient taking photos of my "Rugs" as he so lovingly calls them.

Helen Young for all of her help.

Moneca Calvert for keeping me together.

And the rest of you for your love and encouragement: Michael Spencer, Eddie Hogan, Hans Ingebretson, Sonya Barrington, Lola, "The Burger," Scott and Damon, Judy and Judy, Herb and DeLoris, Gail, Mark, Cathy and Tom, Pam and Larry, Richard, Janet, Debbie, Cynthia, Bonnie, Marsha, Daye, The Redwood Empire Quilters Guild, and EGA Humboldt Chapter...

Thank You

I began quiltmaking quite by accident. I have lived in Eureka, California all of my life except for five short months. Those five months were spent in Woodside, California with my Aunt and Uncle. My mother was ill and needed treatment in San Francisco, and I was playing the role of nurse. To fill my idle time, I took a few classes at the local community college. An embroidery class was on my agenda. After the second class, I learned that it was not an embroidery class, but a quilting class. After being convinced I should complete at least a small quilt, I took heed and pieced my first sampler quilt in 1977 from a suitcase of old scraps. As the class went on, I completed two bed quilts and several lap quilts for Christmas presents. Upon returning home with my mother, I decided Eureka needed a quilt shop and opened "Katie's Quilt Shoppe" in 1978, at the age of 22. With no business knowledge and the little quilting I had done to that point, I ran my little shop, gaining knowledge with each patron's question.

In the summer of 1979, I took a workshop from Michael James, to whom I give all credit and thanks for opening the doors for me again. I had an art background dating back to early childhood. I had worked in many different mediums (watercolors, ink and oils), experimenting with anything I could get my hands on. I had gotten completely away from any form of self expression for three years, during which I was making traditional quilts and running my shop. Michael helped me realize my talent in the art field could be combined with my love of fabrics, their colors and textures. The piece I completed from that workshop is *Starting Point* (plate 1a).

FOREWORD . . . .

The discovery of mandala designs happened one day while I was designing a quilt. I had become tired of working with the traditional square as my repeat motif and began working with triangles. The triangles rotated around a center. I then worked out the basic division of 4, 8, 3, 6 and 5, and how they needed to fit into the whole of 360°. This is a simple technique that will be explained in detail in Chapter II.

The actual mandala design is very structured; however, within that structure you can be very free. That is why anyone can design a mandala. I began teaching mandala design early in 1981. Students came to the workshops sure that they couldn't design their own quilt. After taking them through the basic structure of the mandala and allowing them to design freely within this structure, they were surprised with the results.

As quiltmaking, teaching and lecturing began taking up my time, I started to lose interest in my shop. In the summer of 1982 I sold it to another local quilter. With my time finally my own, I began to develop the mandala design even further.

In June of 1983, my brothers, Tom, Chris and Mark, agreed to help make the fantasy of *Mandala* become a reality. So here we are . . .

I designed this book for everyone. The novice or first-time quilter can pick up this book and, by following the step-by-step instructions, create a beautiful whole-cloth or pieced mandala quilt, while the advanced quilters can use this book to expand their abilities as quilters and begin to design their own quilts in a new and fascinating way.

In the following chapters, I will take you step-by-step through the unique process of design. You may follow the directions step-by-step, just read and absorb, or enjoy the pictures and illustrations. Relax and enjoy and let your creativity flow. All your fantasies can become realities. . .

Mandala designs can be used in many mediums. They are perfect for stained-glass work, woodwork, graphics of all kinds, and just fun doodling.

The mandala is a symbol for centering
and that following one's images inevitably
leads one to his own center.
— C.G. Jung

INTRODUCTION

INTRODUCTION . . . .

Man da la (mun'da la) n. A graphic cosmic symbol shown as a square within a circle, bearing representations of deities arranged symmetrically, and used as a meditation aid by Buddhists and Hindus; in the terminology of the Swiss psychologist, Carl Jung, 1875-1961, a symbol depicting the endeavor to reunite the self.

This is a typical dictionary definition of the mandala. Mandalas are used in many cultures and designs. In my search for the meaning of the mandala, I have encountered many interpretations. Again and again, I run into the word center. The center is the beginning of the mandala. In the Sanskrit, mandala means circle and center. Traditional mandalas consist of a circle, which is the symbol of the cosmos, and the square, the symbol of the earth. A mandala consists of a series of concentric forms suggestive of a passage between different dimensions.

The mandala is a design that is easily understood and enjoyed by the eye and mind. In using the mandala in contemporary design, the principles are the same as the ancient design: an important center with equal sections radiating from that center. In traditional quiltmaking, a block is used. This single block is repeated to form an all-over pattern. When working with a mandala format, a triangle is used. This single triangle is repeated, rotating around the center to form the all-over pattern or whole. The mandalas on these pages are from many different cultures and serve many different purposes, but all are mandalas.

pocketwatch

Stonehenge

In a statement from *Man and His Symbols,* Carl Jung states, "the mandala serves a conservative purpose, namely to restore a previously existing order. But it also serves the creative purpose of giving expression and form to something that does not yet exist; something new and unique. The second aspect is perhaps even more important than the first, but does not contradict it. For in most cases, what restores the old order simultaneously involves some element of the new creation. In the new order the older pattern returns on a higher level. The process is that of the ascending spiral, which grows upward while simultaneously returning again and again to the same point." This statement relates closely to the connection between traditional quiltmaking and contemporary designing.

The contemporary quiltmaker is helping restore the time-old tradition of quiltmaking. The contemporary and traditional quiltmaker's process is basically the same: the making of templates, marking and cutting of fabric, the piecework, and quilting.

Mandalas also serve the creative purpose of giving expression and form to something that does not exist. Each mandala design is a new design, all are different, and all help to create something new from within.

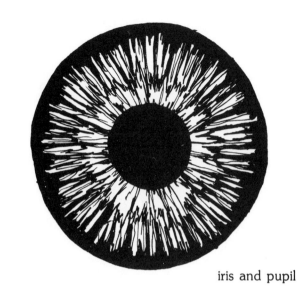

iris and pupil

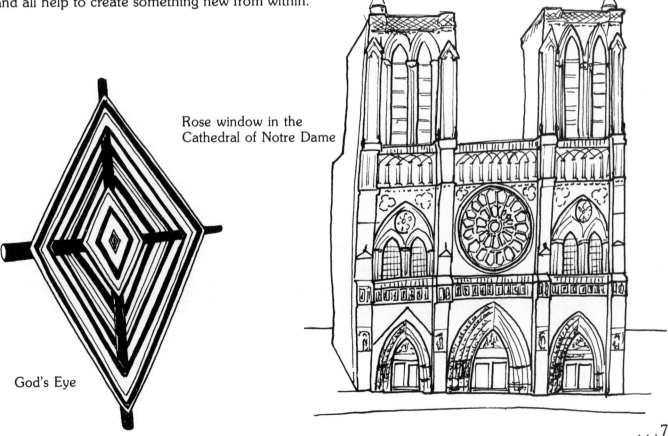

Rose window in the
Cathedral of Notre Dame

God's Eye

A properly drawn mandala is a book in itself containing a great deal of information but he who would read the symbols must learn the language.

—Robert S. De Ropp

I SUPPLIES

SUPPLIES ....

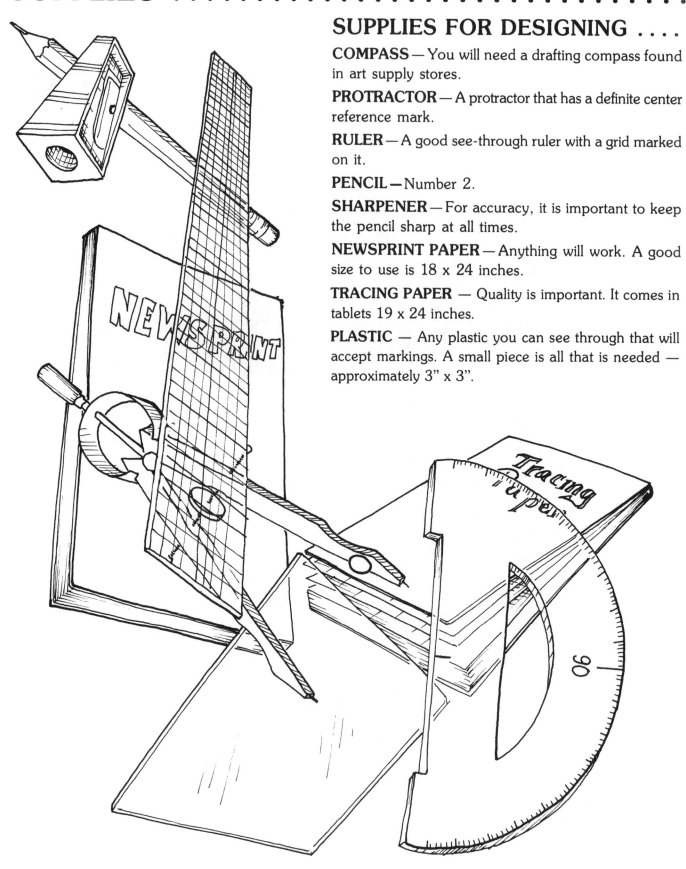

SUPPLIES FOR DESIGNING . . . .

COMPASS — You will need a drafting compass found in art supply stores.

PROTRACTOR — A protractor that has a definite center reference mark.

RULER — A good see-through ruler with a grid marked on it.

PENCIL — Number 2.

SHARPENER — For accuracy, it is important to keep the pencil sharp at all times.

NEWSPRINT PAPER — Anything will work. A good size to use is 18 x 24 inches.

TRACING PAPER — Quality is important. It comes in tablets 19 x 24 inches.

PLASTIC — Any plastic you can see through that will accept markings. A small piece is all that is needed — approximately 3" x 3".

There are many brands of each of these supplies. Shop around to find which brands work best for you.

SUPPLIES FOR SEWING . . . .

MATTE BOARD — A large sheet of matte board for making templates.

X-ACTO KNIFE — For cutting the matte board.

MARKING PENCILS — Water-soluble marking pencils or felt pens for marking the fabric.

SCISSORS — Top quality dressmaker scissors for cutting fabric. Cheap scissors for cutting paper.

PINS — Quilters pins; these are extra long with glass heads.

DRESSMAKERS TRACING PAPER — There are several types out. Be sure to get the chalky kind.

BATTING — Any bonded batting will do. I use a 3 oz. polyester bonded batt.

SEWING THREAD — A good quality thread in the same color range as the fabrics to be sewn.

QUILTING THREAD — Quilting thread the same color or darker than the fabric you are quilting over. I prefer the cotton-covered polyester core.

THIMBLES — Be sure they fit comfortably, but snug.

NEEDLES — Betweens or quilting needles. Size 9 thru 12.

HOOP — A large sturdy quilting hoop.

REDUCING GLASS OR BINOCULARS — For viewing work in progress; look through the wrong end of the binoculars — these make the piece appear further away and blend the colors together.

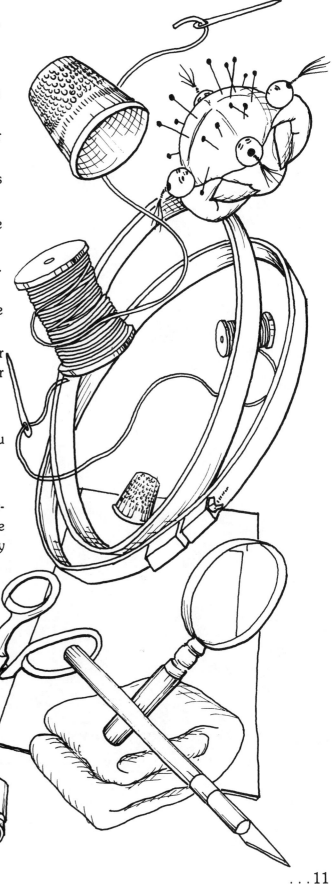

SUPPLIES . . . .

YARDAGES . . . .

WHOLE-CLOTH MANDALAS — 1-5/8 yards of polished cotton, 49 inches wide. This allows enough for binding.

PIECED MANDALAS — Bits of everything from your scraps. When I purchase fabric, I find 3/8 of a yard is enough; not many templates will be larger than that. When I can afford it, I like to buy one yard.

II BASIC DIVISIONS

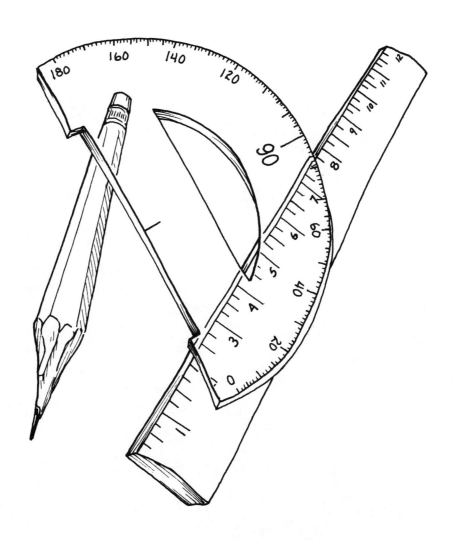

BASIC DIVISION ·

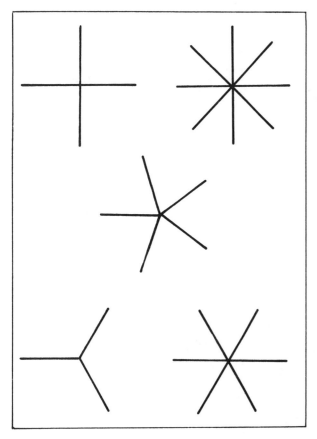

master sheet

All mandalas are made up of equal sections that rotate around a center. All of the sections are made up of equal degrees. The total of these degrees is 360°, or a circle. (Remember, mandala means circle.)

There are five basic divisions to the mandala process. The divisions are:

4 — Four angles each of 90°
8 — Eight angles each of 45°
3 — Three angles each of 120°
6 — Six angles each of 60°
5 — Five angels each of 72°

In this chapter, we will draft these divisions using a protractor and a ruler.

To begin doing mandala designs, you need a master sheet with the five basic divisions drawn on it very accurately.

Using a large sheet of newsprint paper (18 x 24) as your master sheet, begin drafting your divisions.

DIVISION OF 4 · · · · · · · · · · · · · · ·

All of the segments must add up to the whole of 360°. Dividing 4 into 360°, the divisions will each be 90°. Using a ruler and a protractor, begin by drawing a straight line approximately six inches long. (You will want to get all of the divisions on one page. Therefore, be sure to leave enough room for the other divisions.) Mark a small center reference point. Place your protractor on this line with the 0's and center lined up. Make a small mark at 90°. Connect with a ruler the mark at 90° and the center reference, then on through to the other side. Now there are four equal sections of 90° each that together add up to 360°. Label 90°, division of 4.

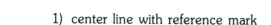

1) center line with reference mark

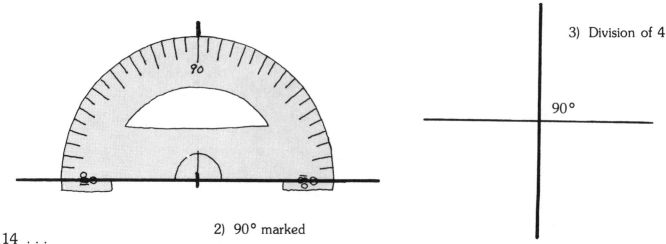

2) 90° marked

3) Division of 4

90°

DIVISION OF 8 . . . .

8 divides into 360° to give you 8 divisions of 45°. Draw a center line and a center reference point. With the protractor, line up the 0's and the center, and mark off units of 45° each. Connect these marks to the center and on through to the other side. Label 45° division of 8.

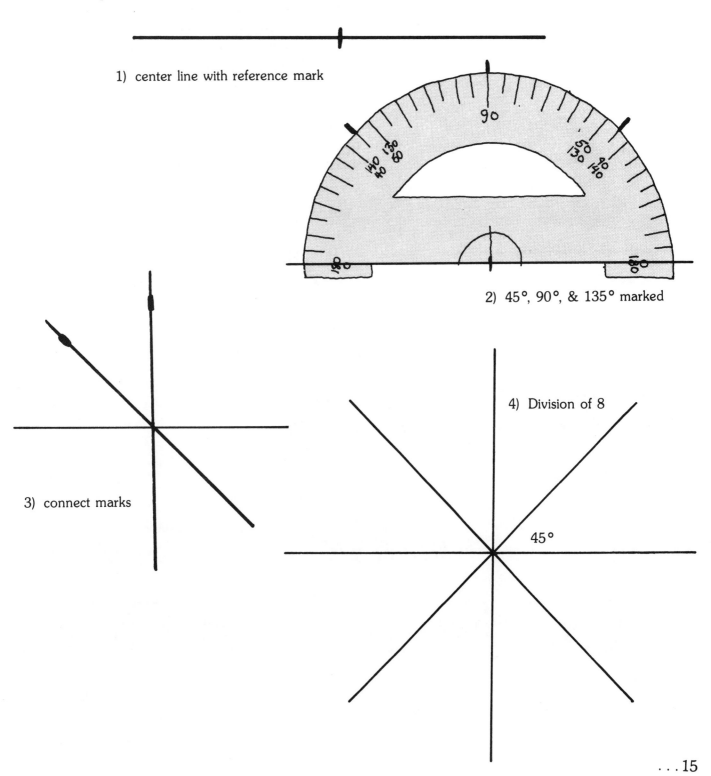

1) center line with reference mark

2) 45°, 90°, & 135° marked

3) connect marks

4) Division of 8

45°

BASIC DIVISIONS . . . .

DIVISION OF 3 . . . .

This begins a little differently than the others, because it is an uneven division. Begin with ½ the center line, with the center reference at the end of the line.

3 divides into 360°, 120 times. The divisions will each be 120°. Place the protractor so the center is on the reference mark and one of the 0's is on the line and mark 120°, (be sure to follow the series of numbers on the inside of the protractor if the 0 you start with is on the inside, or the series on the outside if the 0 is on the outside). Connect that mark to the center reference. Do not cross over the center. Now place the protractor on this second line, matching centers. Mark 120° again. Connect that mark to the center reference. Do not cross over. Label 120° division of 3.

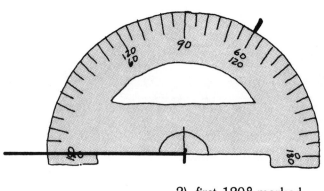

1) ½ center line with reference mark

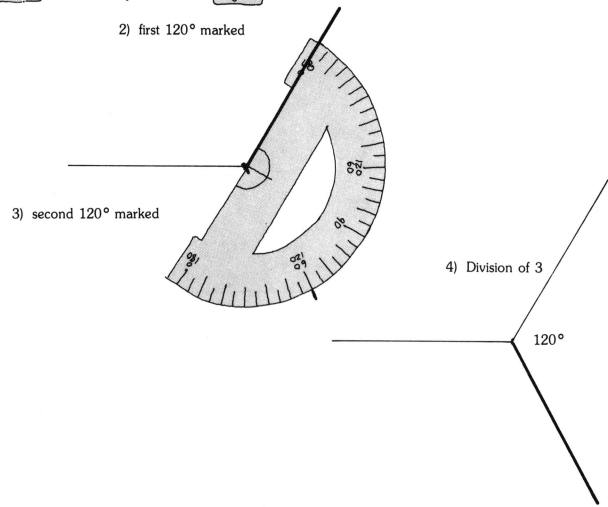

2) first 120° marked

3) second 120° marked

4) Division of 3

120°

DIVISION OF 6 . . . .

6 divides into 360° to give you 6 divisions of 60°. Begin with a center line and the center reference. Place the protractor on this line so the 0's and centers line up, mark 60° and 120°. Connect these marks to the center and on through to the other side. There will be six equal sections of 60° each. Label 60° division of 6.

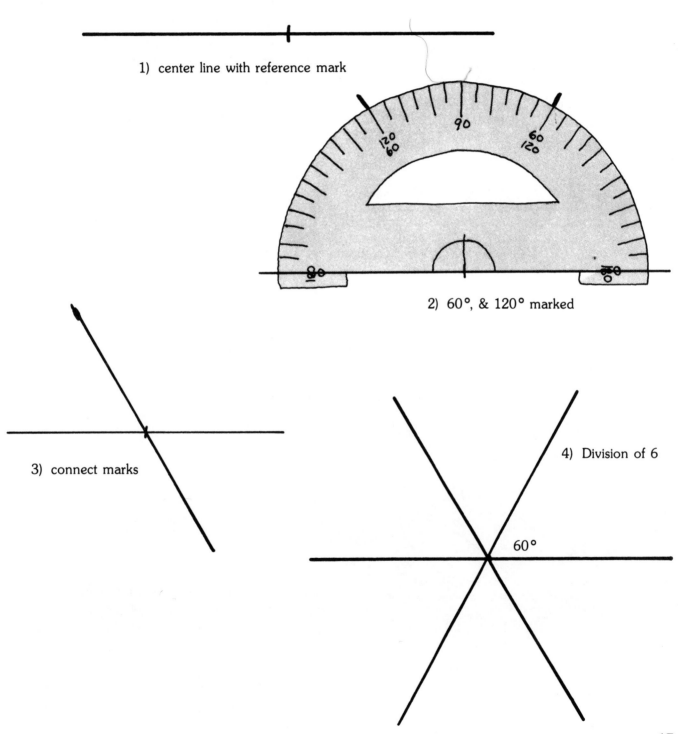

1) center line with reference mark

2) 60°, & 120° marked

3) connect marks

4) Division of 6

60°

BASIC DIVISIONS . . . .

DIVISION OF 5 . . . .

360° divided by 5 is 72°. Once again, this is an uneven division, as is the division of 3. Draw one half the center line with the center reference at the end of this line. Place the protractor with the 0° on the line and the centers lined up. Mark 72° and 144°. Connect these two marks to the center. Do not cross over the center. Place the protractor upon the last line drawn, matching center reference and 0°. Mark 72° and 144°, again. Connect these two marks to the center, and there will be 5 sections of 72°. Mark 72° division of 5.

1) ½ center line with reference mark

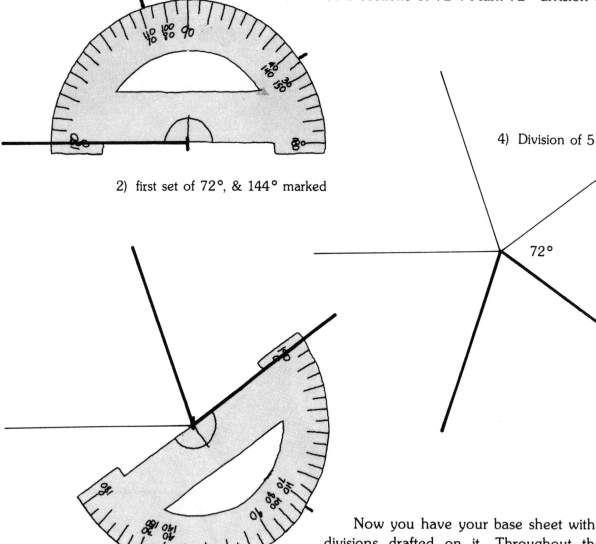

2) first set of 72°, & 144° marked

4) Division of 5

72°

3) second set of 72°, & 144° marked

Now you have your base sheet with the 5 basic divisions drafted on it. Throughout the next few chapters, you will be exploring three avenues of design based on these divisions. The first method uses overlapping circles to create a curvilinear design; the second uses a square template or other shapes; the third by designing directly within one triangular section.

III INTERLOCKING CIRCLES

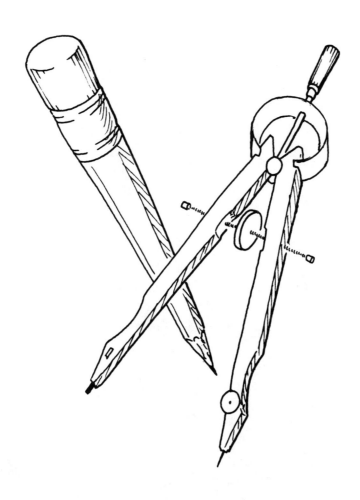

INTERLOCKING CIRCLES ....

The first avenue of design is with circles. Using a compass to create these circles, and the basic divisions as structures to work on, we will create the curvilinear mandala.

The Mandala on this page is created by an overlapping of five circles based on the division of 4. Four arches, or parts of circles, were added to the outside. This is the basic design of my first quilt *Starting Point*, also pictured. (Plate 1a & 1b).

Begin by laying a piece of tracing paper over the base sheet. By drawing only on the tracing paper, the basic divisions will not have to be redrafted each time needed. Using the basic divisions as your guide, begin making overlapping circles on the tracing paper.

EXAMPLE:

Using the division of 4, open the compass to about two inches. Place the point in the center of the division of 4; draw a circle.

Without changing the compass setting, make four more circles by placing the point of the compass where the first circle intersects the four lines from the base division.

At this point, you have a very simple mandala. Any section in itself can be repeated, rotating around the center to get this same design. For a true mandala, the sections are the same; equal sections revolving around the center, that as a whole make up 360°.

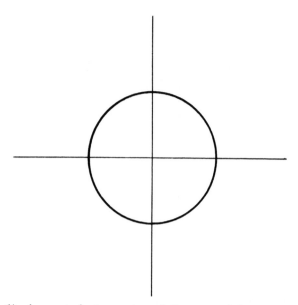

1) draw circle in center of division of 4

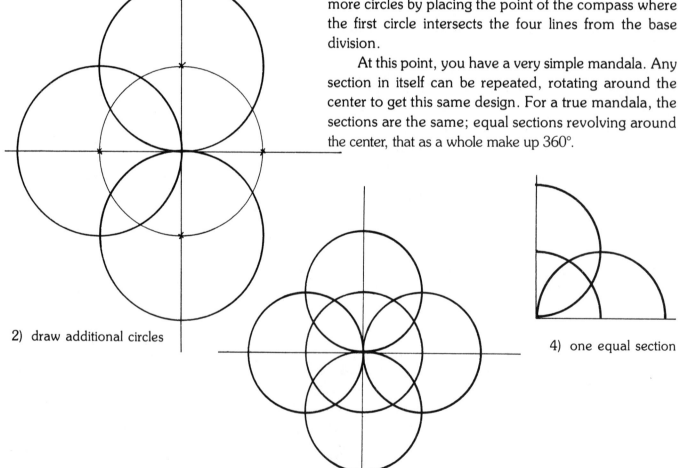

2) draw additional circles

3) simple mandala

4) one equal section

When you move the tracing paper, eliminate the base lines. If you prefer the design with lines, just add them on to your tracing paper.

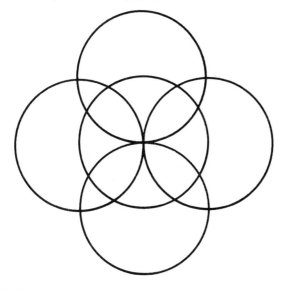

. . . .

Continue using your tracing paper to explore other possibilities of interlocking circles. You may wish to change the size of your circles within any one design, or possibly not make complete circles, just arcs. Here are some examples of these other possibilities of interlocking circles based on the division of 4. (The little lines indicate where the point of the compass was placed.) In each of these drawings the four lines may be eliminated.

DIVISION OF 4

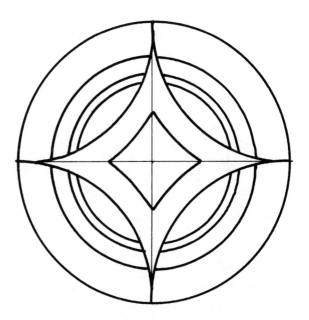

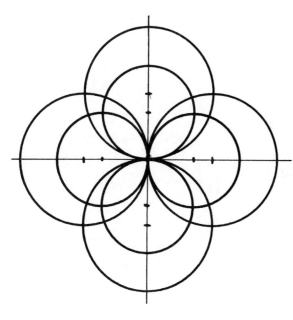

There are thousands of possibilities; this type of designing is limitless. The most important thing to remember is to relax and let your mind wander freely over your paper. Play with it and see what happens. When you feel you have exhausted your possibilities for the time being (you could go on with this for days), try the same process on the other basic divisions. On the following pages, you will find some of these possibilities.

INTERLOCKING CIRCLES ....

DIVISION OF 8

DIVISION OF 3

DIVISION OF 6

DIVISION OF 5

At this stage the designs should be kept fairly simple.
Later, using filler patterns (chapter V and VI), you will
intensify the space. Do not overwork your designs. Try
to be free and open.

Circles
triangles   squares
rotating   interweaving   absorbing
intriguing   designs   from   within
Mandalas
—Randi and Katie

IV INTERLOCKING SQUARES

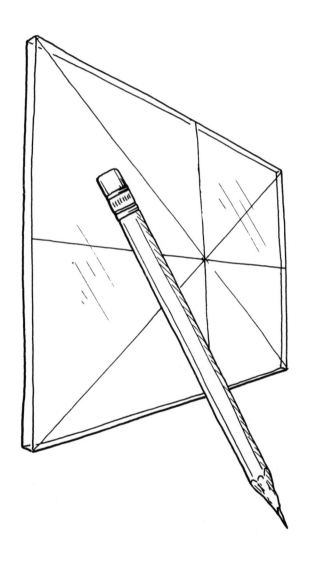

INTERLOCKING SQUARES . . . .

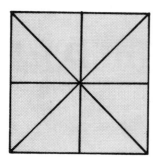

1) plastic template

The second avenue of design involves a square for a more angular design. The square will be used in the same manner as the circle to create interlocking squares.

You will need to make a 2 inch square template. (I prefer to use transparent plastic so that I can see through to my basic divisions.) Divide the square in half by marking corner to corner. Also mark the square vertically and horizontally.

These markings will help line the template up with the basic divisions. Where the lines intersect will be treated the same as the center of the compass. The lines marked should line up with the lines from the basic divisions on the master sheet.

Begin by laying a piece of tracing paper over the basic division of 4. Using the square template as you did the compass, make overlapping squares.

EXAMPLE:

Line the square up with the center of the division of 4 and trace around the template.

Set the square template on the diagonal with the point in the center and draw four more squares.

This will result in a very simple mandala, using the square as your interlocking shape.

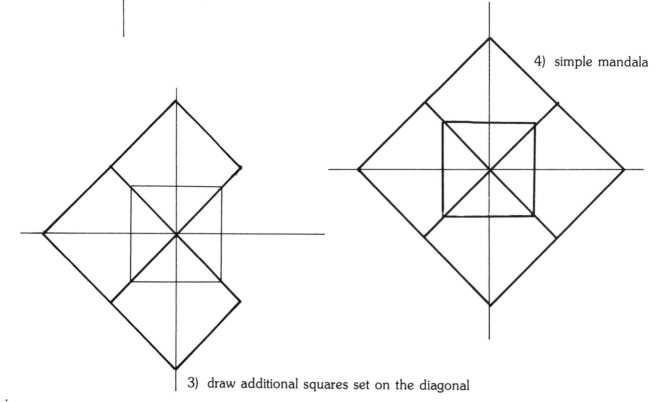

2) draw square in center of division of 4

4) simple mandala

3) draw additional squares set on the diagonal

Continue experimenting with the division of 4 using the square template. Then move on to the other divisions.

DIVISION OF 8

DIVISION OF 4

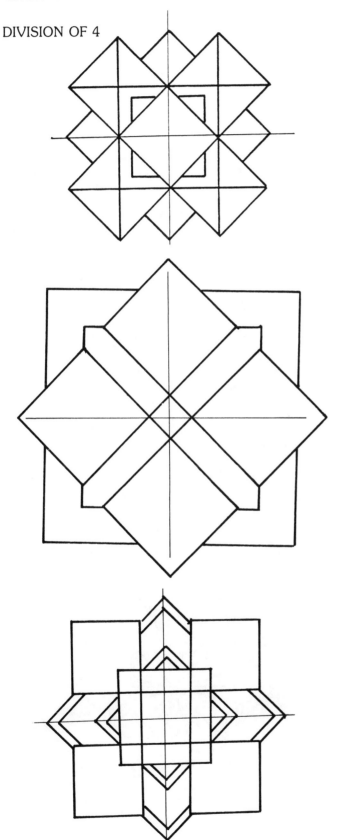

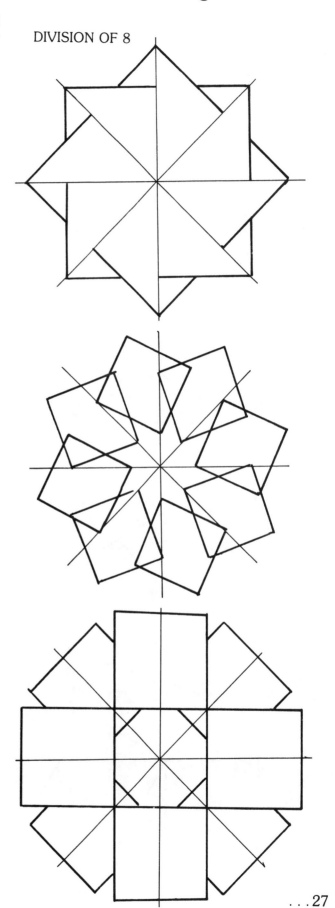

INTERLOCKING SQUARES . . . .

DIVISION OF 3

DIVISION OF 6

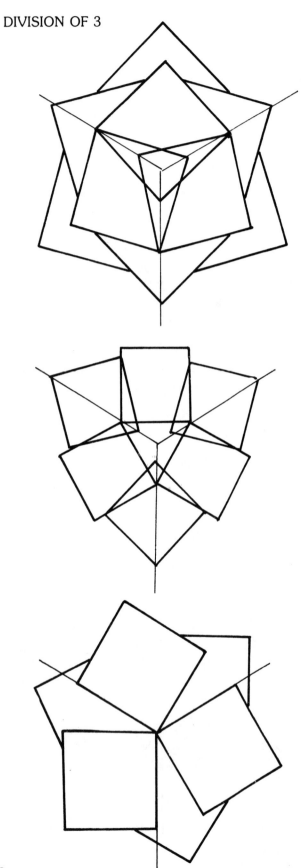

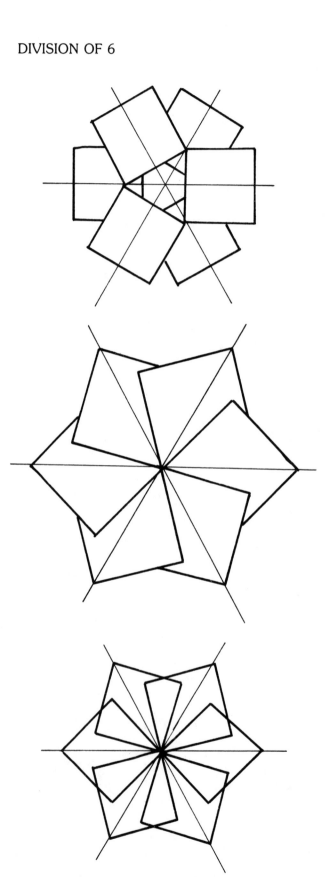

.................INTERLOCKING SQUARES

You may wish to try other shapes besides a square. Some possibilities might be hearts, flowers, diamonds, rectangles, etc. Set up your designs in the same manner using the basic divisions. Remember to have fun!

DIVISION OF 5

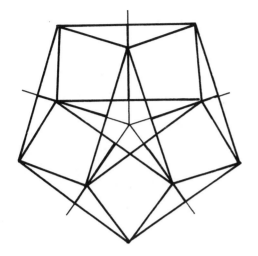

OTHER POSSIBILITIES

Hearts by Moneca Calvert

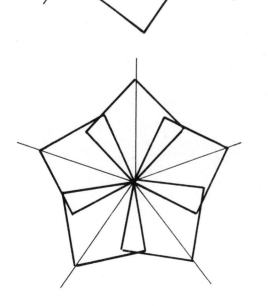

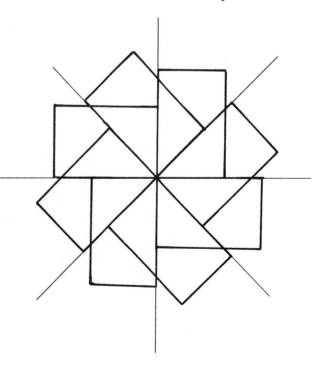

"We know from experience that the protective circle the mandala, is the traditional antidote for chaotic states of mind."

—C.G. Jung

Archetypes of the Collective Unconscious

V TRIANGLE UNITS

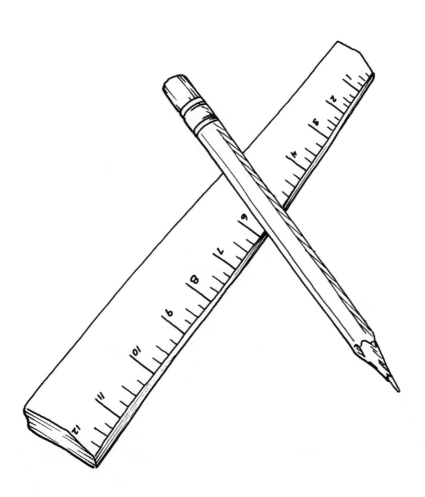

TRIANGLE UNITS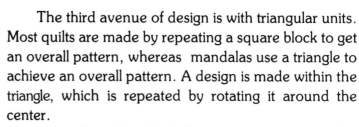

The third avenue of design is with triangular units. Most quilts are made by repeating a square block to get an overall pattern, whereas mandalas use a triangle to achieve an overall pattern. A design is made within the triangle, which is repeated by rotating it around the center.

You will work in the following manner: Trace the angle from any of the basic divisions. Playing with straight lines and curves within this triangle, create a simple design. Repeat this design to get a more interesting mandala.

EXAMPLE:

Begin by taking a sheet of tracing paper. Lay it over any of the basic divisions. Trace only one of the angles.

Check this angle with your protractor to be sure it is the proper degree. Remove the tracing paper and lay it on a clean sheet of paper so that there are no conflicting lines.

Play with lines inside this triangle unit. (Do not worry how the entire design will turn out, just play). You may wish to draw a few lines to get started. Use a ruler.

Then you may enclose the outside edge.

By relaxing and playing with lines, break the large areas down into smaller areas of more interest.

Keep it simple at this point, because we will be going into more detail with filler patterns later.(See chapter V)

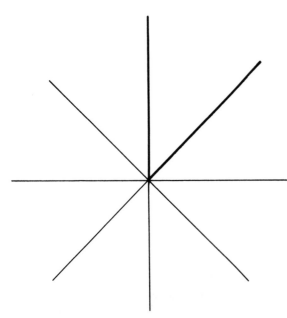

1) one division of 8 angle traced

3)

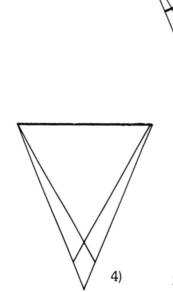

4)

2)

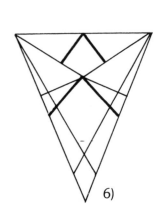

5)

6)

2-6) play with lines within the triangle unit

32...

Is it difficult to tell whether this will be a good design or not? The only way to tell is by repeating the pattern. Normally the way a quilt is made is with a repeat of a square block. Remember mandalas are done with a repeat of a triangular shape, rotating around an all important center. You have the triangle, now you need to repeat it.

To do this, take another piece of tracing paper, lay it over the triangle design and trace it. Then turn the tracing paper and trace your design again so that centers and angle lines match up.

Repeat this process the number of times needed to complete the design.

Things will begin to happen that weren't apparent from the original triangle alone. Note the difference between figures 6 and 7. Lines will begin to interact to form a more complicated design. Some lines may need to be erased in order to have a clearer design.

In this design, I erased all the lines within the long points. You may wish to add lines as well as erase them. I finished this design off by adding the outside edge.

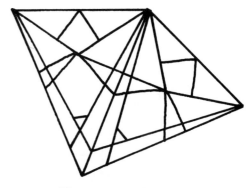

7) a repeat of two triangle units

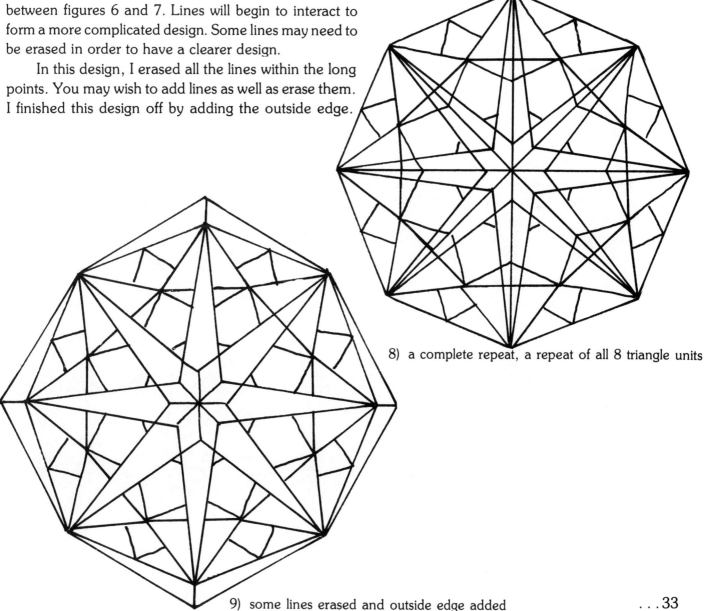

8) a complete repeat, a repeat of all 8 triangle units

9) some lines erased and outside edge added

...33

TRIANGLE UNITS ....

Here are some examples of triangle units on the
different divisions.

DIVISION OF 4

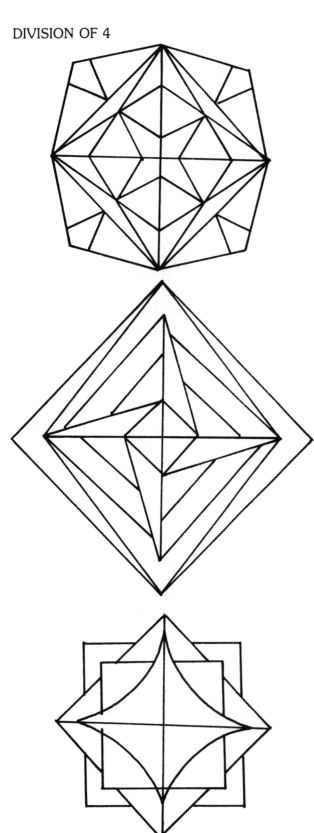

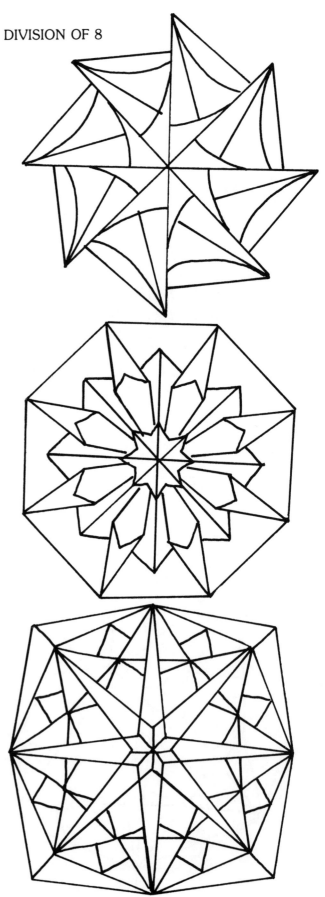

34 . . .

DIVISION OF 3

DIVISION OF 6

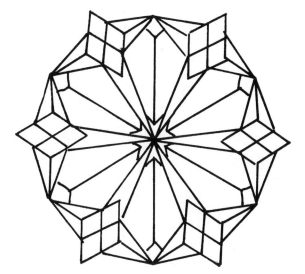

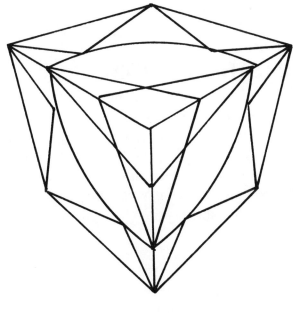

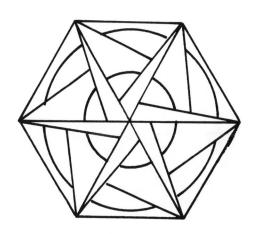

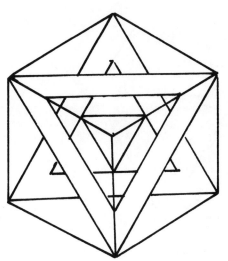

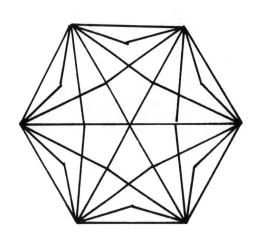

TRIANGLE UNITS

DIVISION OF 5

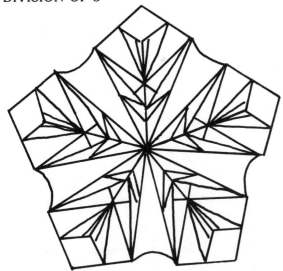

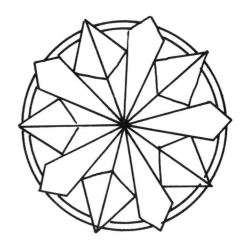

ASYMMETRIC DESIGNS . . . .

If you are working with an asymmetric design (one that is not equal on both sides) within a triangle unit there will be another possibility: flipping the design. This is only possible on the even divisions of 4, 6, and 8. First repeat this section by tracing it face up within the divisions as we have done before, repeating it the number of times needed to complete the design.

1) an asymetric triangle unit

2) triangle unit repeated 6 times face up

To get a different design from the same original triangle you will need to flip it. Begin by tracing the triangle in every other section as shown. Then turn the triangle unit that you are tracing over and fill in the empty sections. You will be surprised at the difference in the two designs. Compare figure 2 with figure 4. This will only work with asymmetric designs in the triangle and on even divisions.

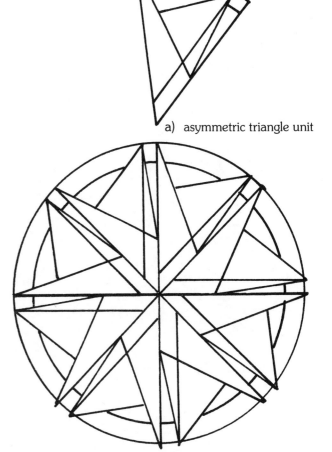

a) asymmetric triangle unit

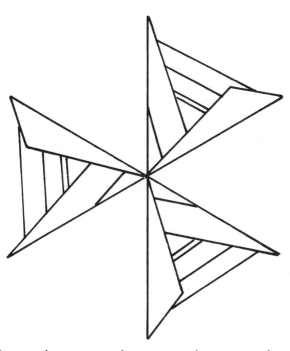

3) triangle unit traced in every other section face up

b) triangle unit repeated 8 times face up

c) triangle traced alternating face up and flipped in alternating sections folded newsprint

4) triangle unit flipped and traced in empty sections

TRIANGLE UNITS ....

I work mainly with geometric patterns. If you are fond of appliqué and wish to work with this type of method, mandala designs adapt nicely. Draw your free-line design in one of the triangle units. Repeat it. You will get a kaleidoscopic effect.

38...

VI FILLER PATTERNS

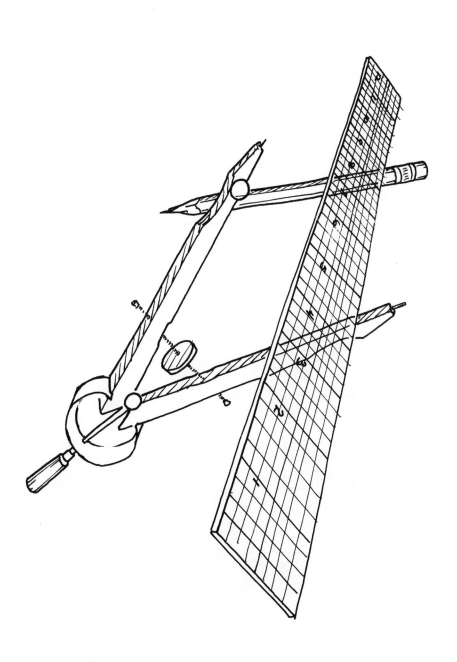

FILLER PATTERNS . . . .

Filler patterns are made up of series of lines and curves that enhance the design. You can make a more effective design by closely quilting some areas with filler patterns and leaving other areas unquilted. This adds a special relief to the design.

This chapter on filler patterns is just a design exercise and should be treated as such. It should be worked with an open mind and quickly for the most spontaneity. I have given examples. Please try some of your own designs.

Take a piece of newsprint and fold it so there are 16 units to work within. The units should be at least 4 x 6 inches.

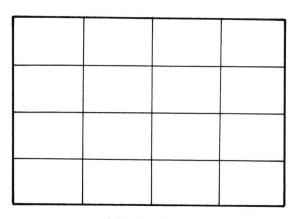

folded newsprint

GRIDS . . . .

In the first box, make a basic grid equal distance apart, using a pencil and ruler, filling the box. (A basic grid is a set of lines that cross vertically and horizontally on a 90° angle.)

In the next two boxes, draw variations on the basic grid. Keep these lines crossing on a 90° angle vertically and horizontally. Next, draw a diagonal grid where the lines still cross at 90°.

Now try a diagonal grid where the lines cross at a tighter angle, so that instead of squares, a more diamond shape will emerge.

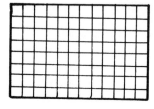

basic grid

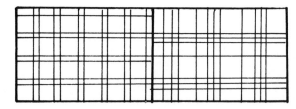

variations of the basic grid

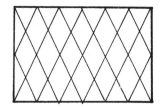

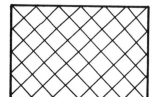

diagonal grids

RADIATING PATTERNS . . . .

Place a dot in the center of the next unit and radiate from it to the outside edge.

Now, place a dot in opposite corners and radiate from these points to the outside edge. The lines will cross, creating a different type of grid.

Place a dot in two adjacent corners and radiate from these creating an even different grid.

CURVED LINES . . . .

Fill the next unit with concentric circles. (Concentric circles are circles that all have the same center.) Using a compass make concentric circles that are equal distance apart.

Then try concentric circles that are an unequal distance apart.

Now, place two dots in diagonally opposite corners and make a curvilinear grid by placing the point of your compass on the dots, making quarter circles that fill the box.

Next, place two dots in adjacent corners and make concentric circles that overlap to form an even different grid.

Using the ruler again, try concentric rectangles an equal distance apart, and concentric rectangles an unequal distance apart.

The last two units should be filled with something from your imagination. The page is now filled with possibilities for filler patterns to be used in the next chapter.

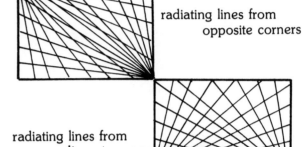
radiating lines from center

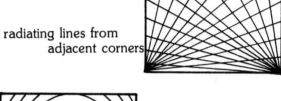
radiating lines from opposite corners

radiating lines from adjacent corners

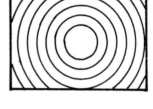
concentric circles

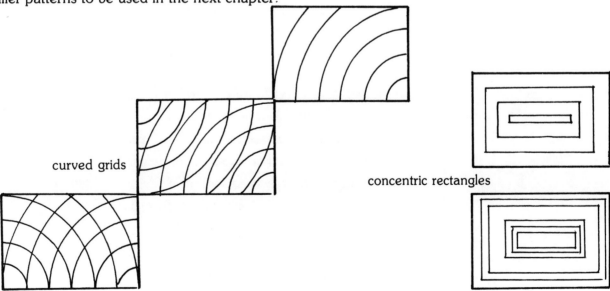
curved grids

concentric rectangles

The mandala is generally depicted as a
circle which revolves around a center,
which signifies that everything around you
becomes part of your awareness, the whole
sphere expressing the vivid reality of life.
                                    —Chogyam Trungpa
        Cutting Through Spiritual Materialism

VII FILL-IN DESIGNS

FILL-IN DESIGNS ....

Fill-in designs are created by using the ideas from the previous chapter on filler patterns to enhance the simple whole-cloth mandala design. In the whole-cloth quilt, the entire design is achieved by the quilted line. By using filler patterns to fill certain areas, you create a more intricate design. You will find some areas need to have closely quilted filler patterns to make other areas puff out. By using polished cotton, the quilted lines will be enhanced by the way the light is reflected off the polish.

Go through all of your designs from the previous chapters and find one that pleases you enough to develop further with filler patterns. Pin the design you wish to develop on the wall, stand back and study it. Decide which areas you want to emphasize. At this point you may wish to eliminate any unnecessary lines to clean up the design or add a few for a better statement.

Now that you have your simple mandala you are ready to enhance it, and make it as intricate as you choose.

Rather than drawing directly on the simple mandala, take another piece of tracing paper and lay it on top and experiment on it. This way if the filler pattern isn't pleasing you can just move the tracing paper and start again, rather than have to erase and ruin your original design.

Try out different types of filler patterns, remembering that you want to leave some areas open (unquilted), and some closely quilted. (Refer back to your newsprint page of filler patterns.)

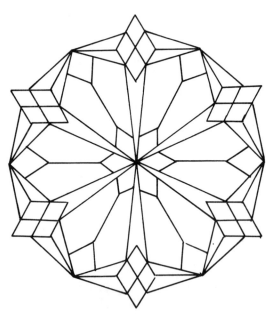

1) simple mandala

2) radiating lines from center

3) radiating lines from outside

44...

In *Crystal Entrapment* (pictured here), I tried out several different types of radiating patterns before settling on a combination of two.

First I tried radiating lines from the center, then radiating lines from the outside, and finally a combination of the two. The combination breaks up the repetition, making the entire design more interesting.

Next, I added a grid in the diamond shape (drawing #5). I chose to put the grid in the outside and inside diamonds rather than the two side diamonds, because the outside edges need to have some quilting in order to keep their shape and hang properly.

Finally, I added some more radiating lines on the outside shapes.

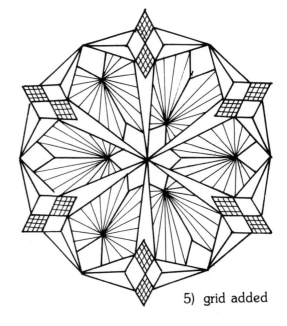

5) grid added

4) a combination of the two previous radiating patterns

6) a complete mandala

FILL-IN DESIGNS ....

Here are some examples of other designs with filler patterns added.

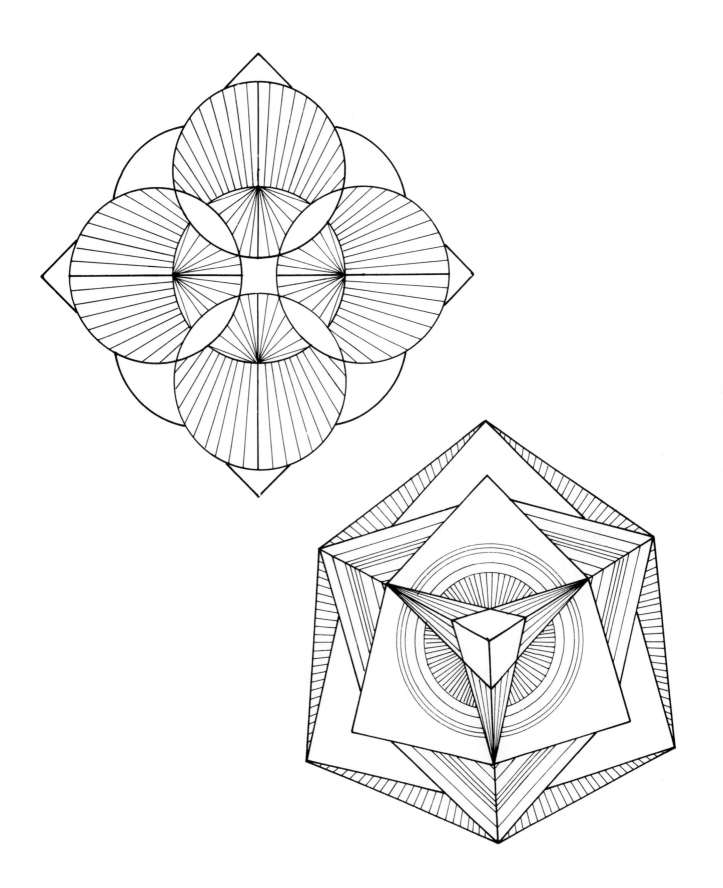

FILL-IN DESIGNS ....

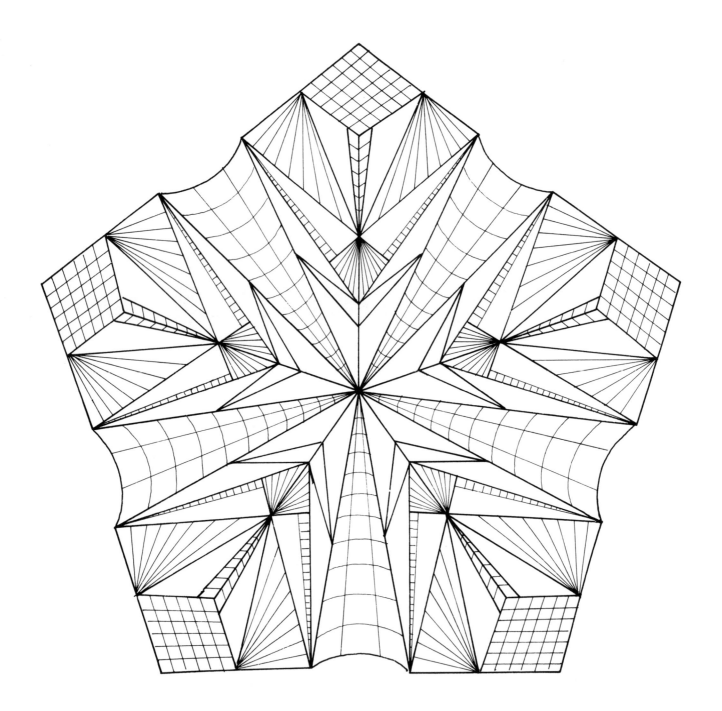

Once you are satisfied with your filler patterns, redraw them on the original design; then study the design again to see what more it needs. Leave your mind open and let the design guide you in your next decision.

When the design is complete and there is a balance between tightly quilted areas and unquilted open areas, you are ready to enlarge and mark the design on the fabric.

VIII ENLARGING

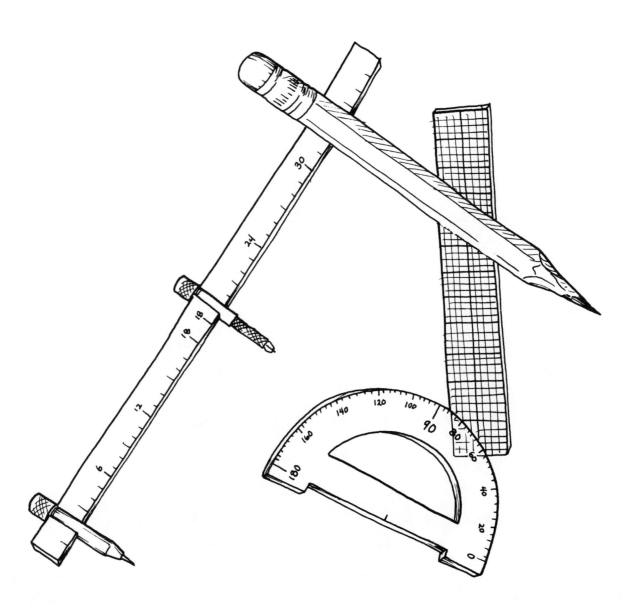

ENLARGING . . . .

To change from a small drawing to a full-size pattern, you must enlarge one section of the design. Only one section need be enlarged, since the mandala is based on a repeat of that section.

Mark on your paper the section to be enlarged.

The most important thing is to draft that first angle accurately on a larger sheet of newsprint. This angle needs to be exact so that all of the sections will fit together to make the whole. Draw a line at the bottom of the newsprint and mark the end. Using the protractor, line it up on the line, center the mark with the center of the protractor, and carefully mark your angle. Connect this mark to the center.

It cannot be stressed enough how important it is to get this angle accurate. If you are working with the division of 4, as we are doing here, and your angle is 88° instead of 90°, then by the time you repeat this angle 4 times, you are multiplying that 2° inaccuracy by 4, and will be off 8°. It is most important to check this angle; do so by marking 10″ out on both lines. Connect those two points with a line forming a triangle.

1) the section marked to be enlarged

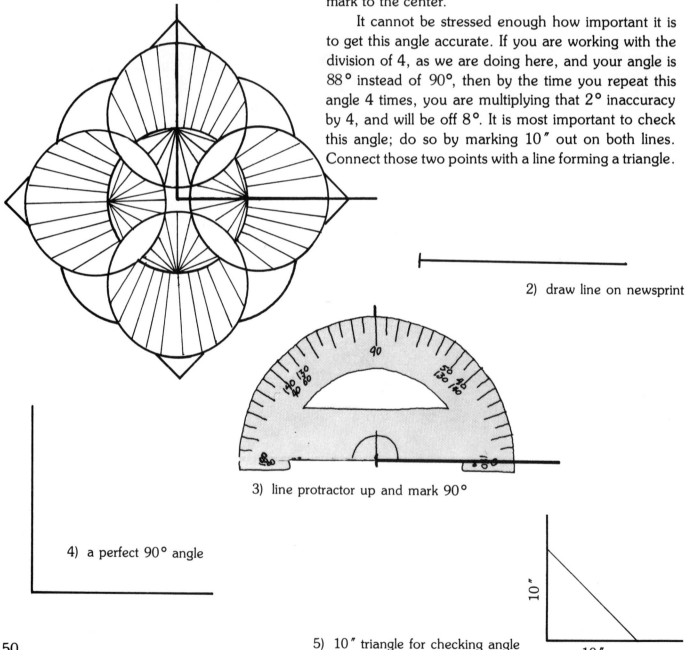

2) draw line on newsprint

3) line protractor up and mark 90°

4) a perfect 90° angle

5) 10″ triangle for checking angle

10″

10″

Check these two angles, they should be the same as each other, and the three angles used to make this little triangle should all add up to 180°. This way of double checking works with all of the divisions. Subtract your center angle from 180°, then divide that number in half to find what the double check angles should be.

DIVISION OF 4

90° center angle
180° minus 90° equals 90°
90° divided by 2 equals 45°
The double check angles should be 45°

DIVISION OF 8

45° center angle
180° minus 45° equals 135°
135° divided by 2 equals 67½°
The double check angles should be 67½°

DIVISION OF 3

120° center angle
180° minus 120° equals 60°
60° divided by 2 equals 30°
The double check angles should be 30°

DIVISION OF 6

60° center angle
180° minus 60° equals 120°
120° divided by 2 equals 60°
The double check angles are 60°

DIVISION OF 5

72° center angle
180° minus 72° equals 108°
108° divided by 2 equals 54°
The double check angles are 54°

Be sure to double check these angles now to avoid problems later.

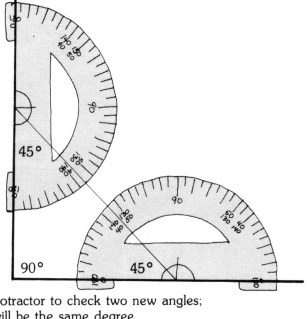

6) use protractor to check two new angles; they will be the same degree

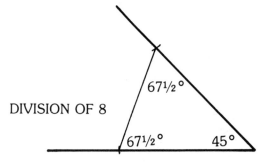

DIVISION OF 8

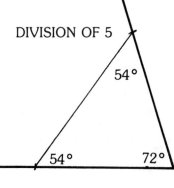

DIVISION OF 5

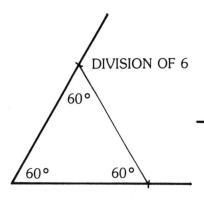

DIVISION OF 6

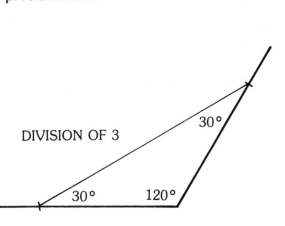

DIVISION OF 3

ENLARGING . . . .

Determine how much to enlarge the section. You are limited by the size of the fabric. To avoid having a seam in a whole-cloth piece, the total size cannot be any larger than the width of the fabric you choose.

If you are using polished cotton, it usually comes in 49″ widths. Figure the piece to be no larger than 44″ across. This gives several inches all the way around the design for cushion. The section being enlarged is half of your design from center to the outside edge. Half of the polished cotton is 22″ so the two lines already drawn on the newsprint need to be 22″ or less.

Measure your design from the center to the edge. If the drawing on the newsprint is 6″ (round this figure if needed for more ease in calculating, for example, 6⅛ rounded off to 6″) and the finished design can be no more than 22″ the ratio would be 3⅔. This was arrived at by dividing the finished size (FS) by the drawing size (DS). This gives the ratio.

$$\frac{FS}{DS} = R$$

$$\frac{22″}{6} = 3⅔$$

3⅔ will be a difficult number to work with. To make the ratio more manageable, reduce the number to the next ½″. This changes the ratio from 3⅔ to 3½. 3½ multiplied by the drawing size of 6 gives a new finished size of 21″ which is below the 22″ limit.

$$\frac{21″}{6} = 3½$$

The finished design will be 3½ times larger than the original drawing. Mark 21″ out on the two lines of your enlargement. Continue by drawing all the lines that were on your original design except for the filler patterns. Remember everything is multiplied by the ratio. If you need to make a large circle and do not have a large enough compass you may wish to purchase an inexpensive yardstick compass at an art supply store.

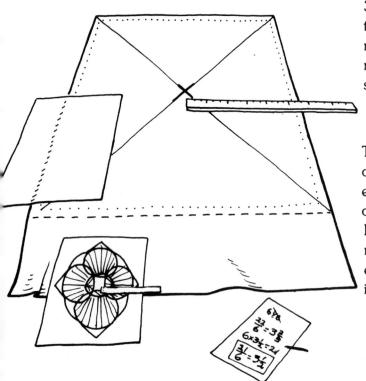

1) find the ratio between drawing size and finish size

EXAMPLE:

If a point of reference is 2″ from the center and the ratio is 3½, then that same point of reference will be 7″ from the center on the enlargement.

If you run into odd fractions round them to an easier number to deal with, just so the enlarged drawing is in good balance with the original.

A common mistake happens when lines that need to meet do not. Avoid this mistake by double checking. Take a long strip of paper and lay it on the edge of the drawing, marking all the lines that need to match. (drawing #1) Then place this piece of paper to the other side (drawing #2), and check to see if they all match. If not, correct.

Now fill in the filler pattern design as it is in your drawing; more or less lines may be needed in your enlargement. If in the small drawing there are five lines to make a radiating pattern, you may find the need for nine lines to fill the same space in the larger drawing. Make the filler pattern proportional.

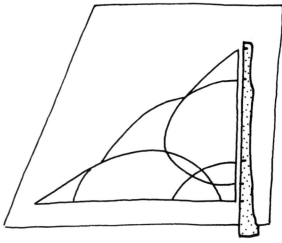

1) mark lines that need to match on a strip of paper

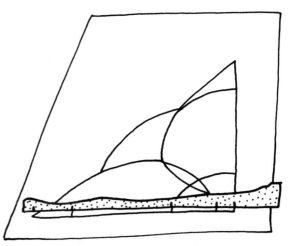

2) move paper to the other side check to see if marks match lines

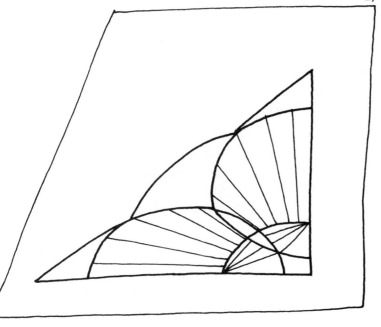

3) add filler patterns

ENLARGING . . . .

If you have tried to figure out the ratio that you will need for your particular design and are a bit confused, if not totally frustrated, don't despair, here is a simple chart with many of the possibilities listed.

In the first column is ½ the drawing size; measure your drawing from the center to the outside edge, find that figure or the one closest to it in this first column. The second column shows how we arrived at the ratios in the third column, the ratio is the multiplication factor showing you how many times larger the finished size will be, which is listed in the last column. The best design size is between 6" and 10". So ½ the drawing size will be 3" to 5" on the chart.

½ Drawing Size	FS/DS = R	Ratio (multiplication factor)	½ Finish Size
2"	22/2 = 11	11x	22"
2 1/4"	22/2.25 = 9.8	9½x	21 3/8" (21.375)
2 1/2"	22/2.5 = 8.8	8½x	21 1/4" (21.25)
2 3/4"	22/2.75 = 8	8x	22"
3"	22/3 = 7.3	7x	21"
3 1/4"	22/3.25 = 6.8	6½x	21 1/8" (21.125)
3 1/2"	22/3.5 = 6.3	6x	21"
3 3/4"	22/3.75 = 5.9	5½x	20 5/8" (20.625)
4"	22/4 = 5.5	5½x	22"
4 1/4"	22/4.25 = 5.2	5x	21 1/4" (21.25)
4 1/2"	22/4.5 = 4.9	4½x	20 1/4" (20.25)
4 3/4"	22/4.75 = 4.6	4½x	21 3/8" (21.375)
5"	22/5 = 4.4	4x	20"
5 1/4"	22/5.25 = 4.2	4x	21"
5 1/2"	22/5.5 = 4	4x	22"
5 3/4"	22/5.75 = 3.8	3½x	20 1/8" (20.125)
6"	22/6 = 3.7	3½x	21"
6 1/4"	22/6.25 = 3.5	3½x	21 7/8" (21.875)
6 1/2"	22/6.5 = 3.4	3x	19 1/2" (19.5)
6 3/4"	22/6.75 = 3.3	3x	20 1/4" (20.25)
7"	22/7 = 3.1	3x	21"
7 1/4"	22/7.25 = 3.0	3x	21 3/4" (21.75)
7 1/2"	22/7.5 = 2.9	2½x	18 3/4" (18.75)
7 3/4"	22/7.75 = 2.8	2½x	19 3/8" (19.375)
8"	22/8 = 2.8	2½x	20"

IX MARKING

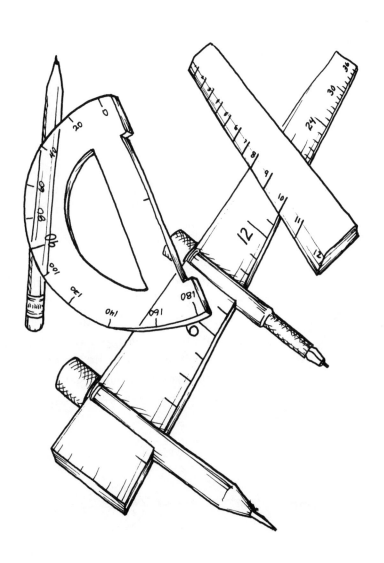

MARKING . . . .

1) cut away excess newsprint from the two sides

Marking is the exciting process of seeing the whole cloth mandala design transformed onto fabric. It is very important to be very accurate. The lines you draw onto the fabric are the lines you will be quilting. If the line drawn is not straight, the quilting will not be straight.

At this point, you should have a piece of newsprint with a section completely and accurately drawn. Cut away the newsprint paper on the lines, leaving the excess at the top. Press your fabric. (I feel that it is not necessary to prewash the fabric if you are going to use this as a wall hanging. If this goes against your grain, then go ahead and wash it.)

Tape your fabric to a flat surface. 1⅝ yards of 49″ polished cotton is sufficient. This gives you enough additional fabric for binding. This piece of fabric is 58½″ x 9″. Of this 9½″ by 49″ will be used for the binding. (Leave this section attached for now. You will trim it off after you are finished quilting.) This will leave a 49″ square. Find the center of that square and mark it with an X from 49″ corner to 49″ corner. Only mark the X in the center.

Once you are set with a center, take your protractor and mark the divisions as we did in chapter I for whatever division you are working with. Mark these divisions with a chalk pencil or erasable fabric marker.

Double check these marks by laying your newsprint pattern on each section, matching to see if all the sections fit. If not, check the angles on the fabric and the pattern to determine what is wrong.

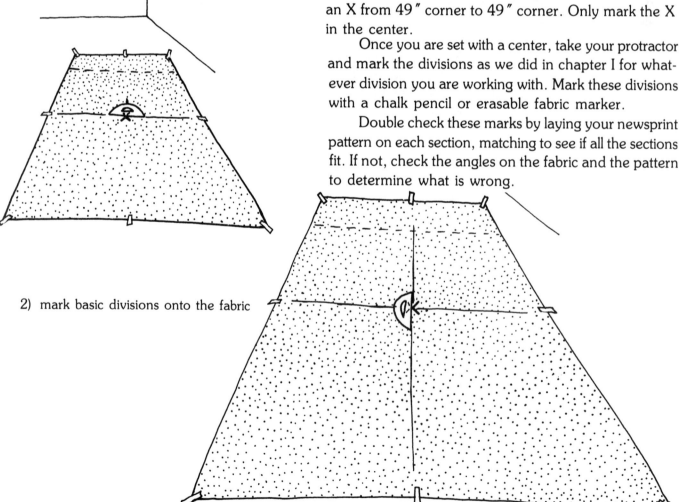

2) mark basic divisions onto the fabric

Now you are ready to transfer all the lines from the pattern onto the fabric, using a good dressmakers tracing paper. (There are several types on the market. Choose the ones with a chalky surface rather than a slick one). Select a color that will be easy to see on the color of polished cotton you are using. Use white for dark colors, blue for light colors.

Line up your pattern with the divisions and pin top and center. Slip the carbon paper between the fabric and transfer all lines. The carbon paper is not as large as a whole section so you will have to mark an area then move the carbon paper to complete the marking. This is a pain but bear with me! (I use an empty ballpoint pen for marking). Use a ruler for straight lines and a compass or yardstick compass for curved lines. After a whole section is marked, move to the next. Before you move the pattern, check to make sure all lines are marked. Remove the center pin, lift up and peek. If you have missed some lines, pin again and complete. Continue until all sections are marked.

3) trace each division using the pattern and dressmakers carbon paper

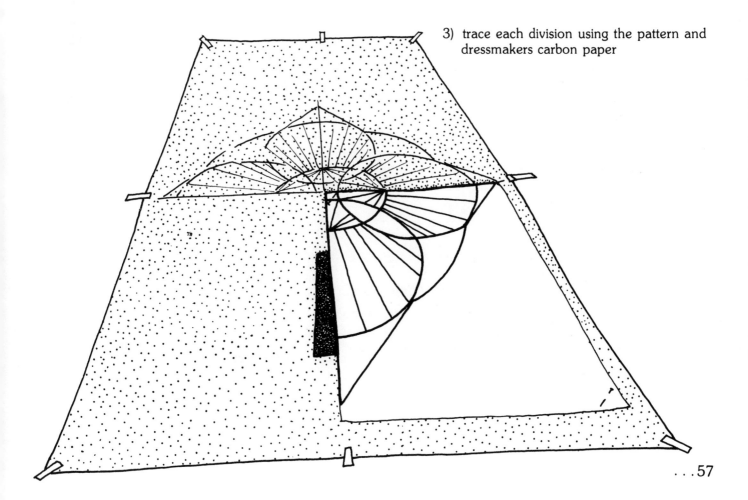

The whole universe is but imagination, all in all, is but a shadow-show of one's own mind.

—Shakespeare

X   PAINTING WITH CLOTH

PAINTING WITH CLOTH . . . .

The mandalas on the next pages were created in one of two ways. The whole-cloth mandala started as a simple line drawing with filler patterns added to create a more complex design. Certain areas are closely quilted, creating intensity, while other areas are left unquilted and appear puffy. These whole-cloth mandalas are all quilted by hand. The pieced mandalas are either a continuation of a whole-cloth mandala (the same pattern interpreted in piece-work), or a new beginning as piecework. Colors were chosen to enhance the design. Light sources in some give added depth; in others, a spatial effect is achieved by the choice of warm or cool colors. In many, a very contemporary shiny fabric, called lamé, was added for accent. The fiber content of each piece varies. These are all wall hangings, so the need for 100% cotton was dismissed. They are all machine pieced and hand quilted. Plates 1a through 14b are all completely done by the author. The last series are by students.

Hue
rainbow   spectrum
splashing   illuminating   radiating
fabric palate of many choices
Color
—Randi and Katie

Plate 1a **STARTING POINT** 44″ x 44″ 1979
This piece was my first original quilt, a starting point for
many more to come. Based on the division of four, the
interlocking circles are enhanced by radiating filler patterns.
The circles resemble fans. The mandala is placed on a grid
background and the border is a repeat of the curves used
in the center.

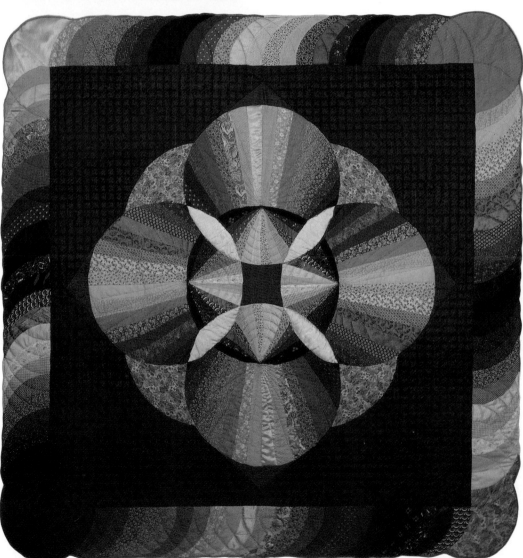

Plate 1b **NOVA** 72″ x 72″ 1980
Many times I work in sets of mandalas, first the whole cloth quilt to experience the design strictly by line,
then the pieced quilt where color and texture come into play. The colors are burgundy (warm) and blue
(cool). The blue background and the blue center circle appear to recede, while the burgundy circles and
points come forward. The border is a combination of both temperatures seeming to undulate around the
quilt. The binding changes colors as it moves around the outside edge. Nova is the point in which a star
reaches its height in brilliance.

Plate 2a **BLAST OFF** 46″ 1980
This piece consists of five equal triangles that rotate around the center. By combining curves, grids and radiating filler patterns with unquilted triangles an exciting explosive design is created.

Plate 2b **HEAVENS REACH** 72″ 1980
Starting at the bottom of this quilt, the red symbolizes the hot core of the earth, the black, the darkness of the underground, with colors then changing to earthtones, to skyblue, sunshine and clouds. The colors, plus the five-sided shape, appear to be reaching upward towards the heavens.

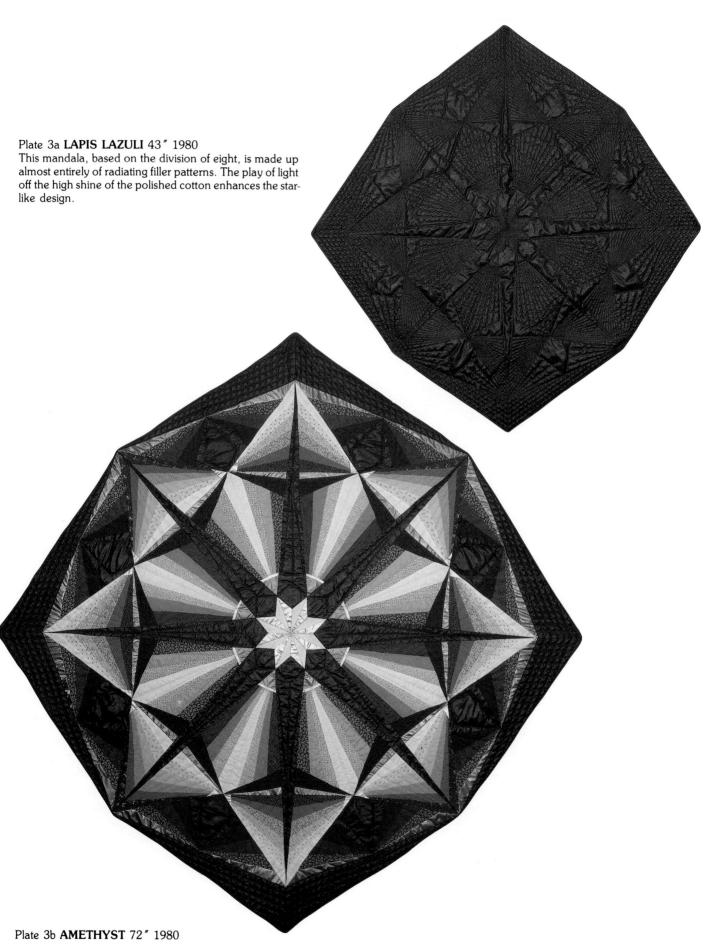

Plate 3a **LAPIS LAZULI** 43″ 1980
This mandala, based on the division of eight, is made up almost entirely of radiating filler patterns. The play of light off the high shine of the polished cotton enhances the star-like design.

Plate 3b **AMETHYST** 72″ 1980
Amethyst appears as a many-faceted stone. The purple lamé sparkles as it catches the light; the gold lamé symbolizes the settings for the stone. The contrast between the pure white polished cotton and the very deep blues and purples make this quilt radiate with light.

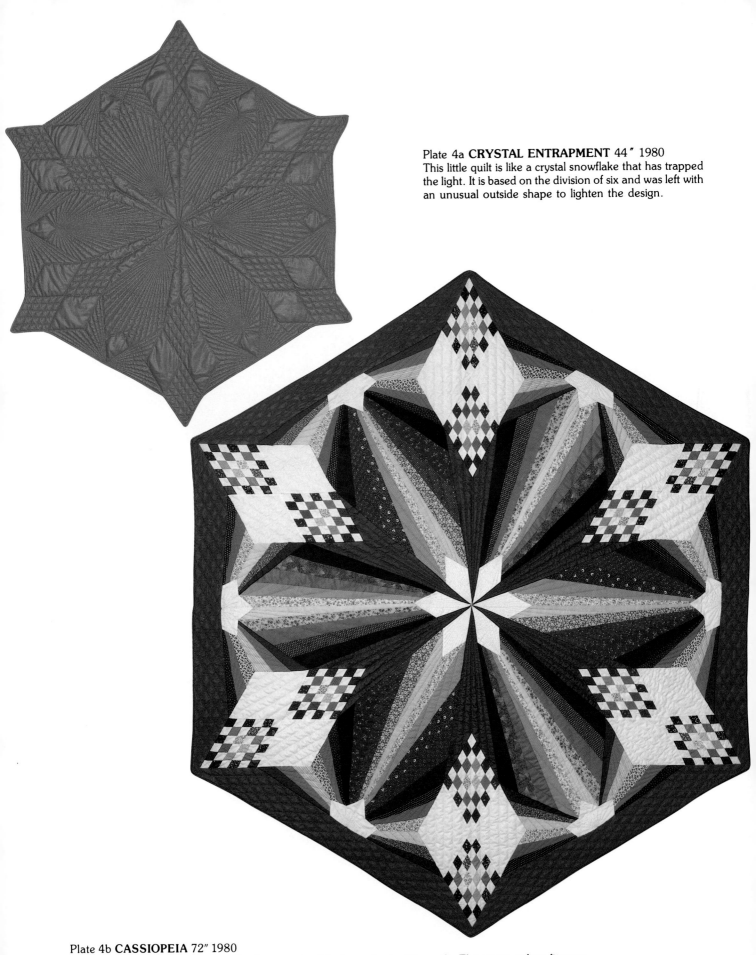

Plate 4a **CRYSTAL ENTRAPMENT** 44″ 1980
This little quilt is like a crystal snowflake that has trapped
the light. It is based on the division of six and was left with
an unusual outside shape to lighten the design.

Plate 4b **CASSIOPEIA** 72″ 1980
A combination of warm and cool colors creates this dynamic star-like quilt. The warm colors fit very
comfortably against the cool blue background. The whole mandala appears to be placed on a burgundy
hexagon that wasn't in *Crystal Entrapment*. According to Carl Sagan's *Cosmos*, Cassiopeia is the
remnant of a supernova. This quilt was made up of the remnants from the quilt *Nova* (1b).

Plate 5 **COSMIC KALEIDOSCOPE** 72″ × 60″ 1980
This wall hanging is made up of many diamond-shaped blocks using Jeffrey Gutcheon's diamond-patchwork method. It was colored to appear as if there were a great light source radiating from the center of the cosmos. The light areas, using warm colors upon a background of cool, move out to the very darkness of the universe. To intensify the celestial feeling, white pearl beads were sewn to the top of the piece to symbolize the constellations. The entire piece is quilted in lines radiating from the center, which help intensify the light source.

Plate 6 **TRON** 54″ 1982
The movie *Tron* inspired the colors for this quilt. The fabrics chosen create a very metallic, computer-like feel to the piece. The mandala design is placed on a navy blue polished cotton and blue lamé disc. The dimensional quality in the quilt causes it to appear as if it were a box with four ovals floating above the blue disc.

Plate 7 **TRON**
Detail

Plate 8 **COLOR WHEEL** 54″ 1981

This quilt is designed to be the fiber workers' color wheel. Starting from the center, there are tints with white added to the six primary colors, which are shown next. Then a wheel of blending colors (colors created by visually mixing adjacent colors); then a strip of lamé for accent. Black, white and grey twirling squares were added for movement. Triangles of the complementary colors were used to round the design. The whole mandala is then placed on a black background and bordered with the six primary colors.

Plate 9 **MELANIE'S ROSE** *72″ x72″* 1982

Melanie's Rose is a study of perspective using a circle. The round circle is drafted to appear as if it is on the side of the boxes, creating a wonderful oval circle. The center of this quilt appears to have a yellow square overlay set on the diamond. The golden circles have turned yellow and the blue background has turned green. Similarly, there is a darker four-point star in the center and along outside areas.

Plate 10 **SPECTRUM** 80″ 1983

Spectrum is actually two quilts that hang as if they were one. The front quilt is made up of many shades of grey, with areas cut away and finished off, through which to view the back quilt. The back piece is made up of the colors of the spectrum in concentric circles, with black and silver beads radiating from the center. The two quilts were blind-stitched together.

Plate 11a **SPECTRUM**
Background quilt.

Plate 11b **SPECTRUM**
Detail

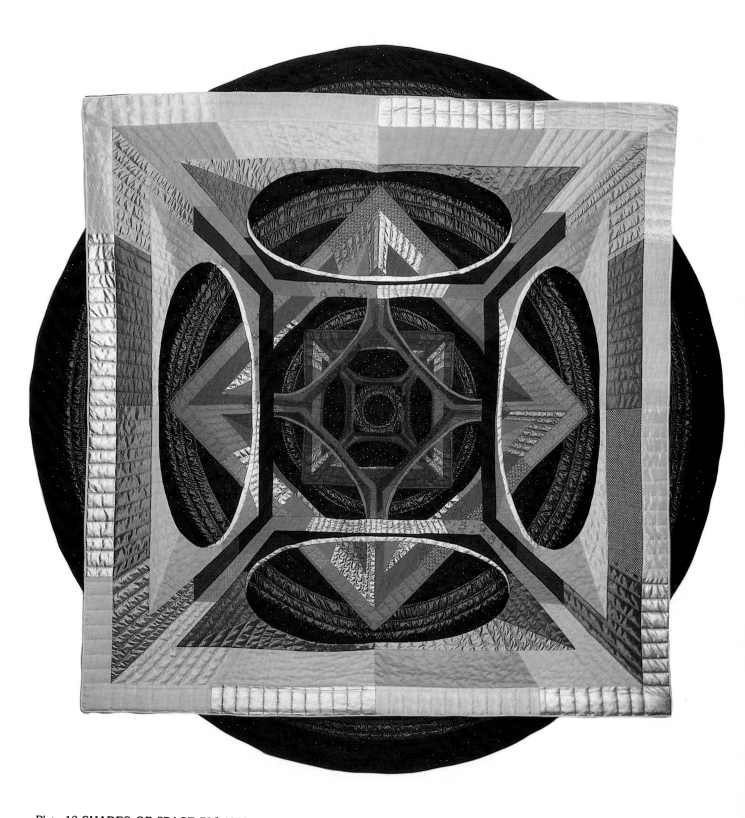

Plate 12 **SHADES OF SPACE** 78″ 1983
Shades of Space starts with three squares traveling away from you in perspective, which are suspended over a black cosmic mandala. This is actually two quilts: the front quilt has the oval spaces cut away to allow you to look through the color into the black "starry night." The back quilt is made up of four types of blacks (100% cotton, polished cotton, satin, and lamé); to this 1,300 little silver beads were sewn to create the stars. The two quilts are suspended from a hollow tube which separates them by six inches, which adds to the depth.

Plate 13a **SHADES OF SPACE**
Background quilt.

Plate 13b **SHADES OF SPACE**
Detail

Plate 14 **CWII** 72″ 1982

Color Wheel II demonstrates the properties of warm and cool colors. The warm ovals (red, orange and yellow) are placed on their complementary cool colors (green, blue and purple). These three sections read true; the oval is on top and the warm colors help make it so. The cool colors are the background, as they should be. In the next three sections the colors are reversed; in these, the oval should still be on top, but because of the cool colors, they fight to recede and the background of warms fights to come forward. The first three sections are calm and read true while the other three seem to fight.

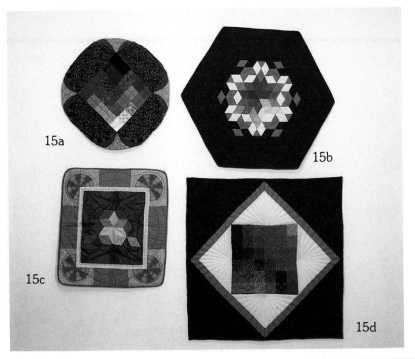

15a
Linda Lillard, Houston, TX, *Color Study I,* 1983

15b
Moneca Calvert, Eureka, CA, *Color Wheel,* 1982

15c
Janet Paluch, Sacramento, CA, *Color Wheel,* 1983

15d
Moneca Calvert, Eureka, CA, *Color Study,* 1982

15e
Janet Paluch, Sacramento, CA, *Color Study, 1982*

15f
Debbie Thompson, Eureka, CA, *Color Windmill,* 1983

15g
Phyllis Derigo, Anaheim, CA, *Emotions in Color,* 1983

15h
Moneca Calvert, Eureka, CA, *Windblown Squares,* 1983

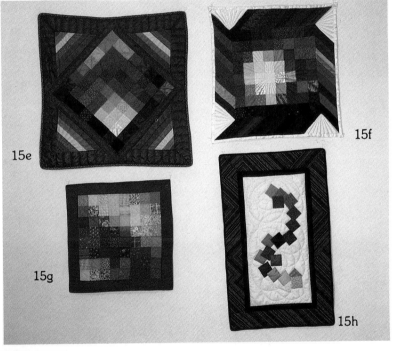

15i
Kim De Coste, Houston, TX, *Crescendo,* 1983

15j
Kim De Coste, Houston, TX, *Color Wheel I,* 1983

15k
Kim De Coste, Houston, TX, *Color Study I,* 1983

Mary Ann Spencer, Eureka, CA, *Star of the Sea*, 1983

Moneca Calvert, Eureka, CA, *Leaves and More Leaves*, 1983

Moneca Calvert, Eureka, CA, *Hearts*, 1982

June Inouye, San Jose, CA, *Mandala (hand painted)*, 1982

XI BASTE, STRETCH, QUILT, AND BIND

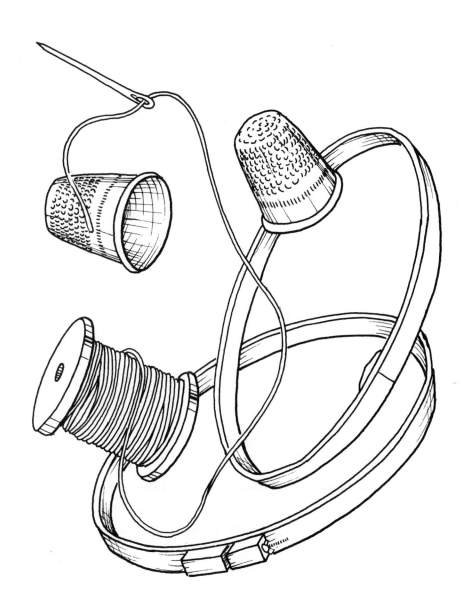

BASTE, STRETCH, QUILT, AND BIND . . . .

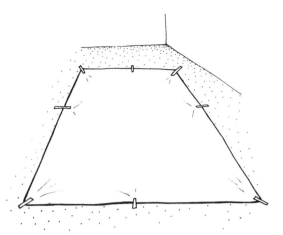

1) tape backing fabric to the floor face down

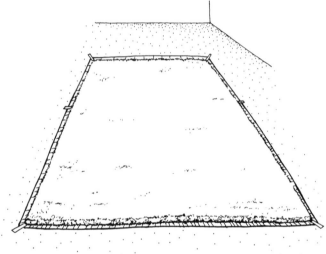

2) lay batting on backing

Basting, stretching, quilting, and binding are the last four steps in the quilting process.

Once your design has been completely marked on your fabric, you are ready to baste your quilt together. You will need three layers: the front has the design marked on it, the center or batting to give loft, and the backing fabric.

Choose a nice fabric for your backing. (I usually use a small calico print of 100% cotton cloth that blends well with the front color and a 3 oz. polyester fiberfill batting.) Place the backing fabric out on a flat surface, a large table or a clean floor works well. Lay it right side down. Using masking tape, secure the fabric evenly and tautly to the flat surface, making sure there are no wrinkles.

Lay the batting on top of the backing fabric, once again making sure there are no wrinkles. Trim away any excess batting, then center the front fabric over these two layers and tape it down. The purpose of basting is to hold the three layers together so that they will not move while you are quilting them.

Baste using a long needle and thread. (I usually baste from the center out, then around the outside edge and center. For a bigger piece, more basting would be needed.) Remove the tape and stretch on the frame.

3) tape front fabric on top and baste all three layers together

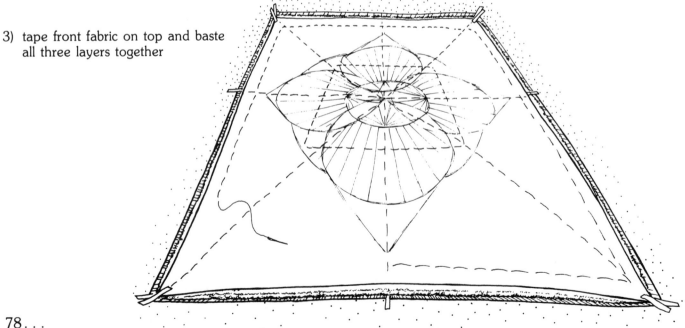

.......BASTE, STRETCH, QUILT, AND BIND

FRAME ....

I work with a 23″ round quilting frame. This looks very similar to an embroidery hoop, only much larger and of a heavier construction.

Always begin working from the center out. Start by placing the inside ring of the hoop under your piece, then place the loosened outside ring on top and push down over the inside ring. Stretch evenly and tautly, then tighten the outside ring.

Before you begin stitching, turn the hoop over, making sure there are no wrinkles on the back side. If there are, stretch them out.

Thread your needle with 12 to 18 inches of quilting thread. Pull the thread off the spool from the side, (not the top), and knot the end you cut to insure less tangles. Choose a color close to the color of the fabric you will be working on. If the right color of quilting thread is unavailable, choose the color you need in regular sewing thread and run it through beeswax to make it as strong as quilting thread.

NEEDLES ....

Use the smallest needle you can work with. They are called "betweens" or "quilting needles." The larger the number, the smaller the needle. Begin by using a 9, then slowly, as you become comfortable, work your way to a 10, and possibly the smallest of all, 12. (The smaller the needle, the smaller the stitch.)

quilt being quilted in hoop

...79

BASTE, STRETCH, QUILT, AND BIND . . . .

QUILTING . . . .

Quilting is a series of small running stitches, the purpose of which is to hold the three layers of cloth together. It creates texture and dimension and should enhance the design (in the whole-cloth quilt, it is the entire design).

The needle goes up and down through the fabric to produce this running stitch. There are many ways to do this. I work from the top, making one stitch at a time. I use two thimbles, one on my middle finger of my right hand to push the needle through the fabric . . . the other on the index finger under the fabric.

Sitting in a comfortable chair, set the quilting hoop on your lap. You will need a thimble on the index finger of your left hand. and a thimble on the middle finger of your right hand. (Reverse left and right if you are left handed.) Push the bottom thimble hard against the quilt in the spot you wish to stitch. With a needle in your right hand, insert the needle through the fabric and glance off the ridge of the bottom thimble. Pull the needle through and repeat. (I do this one stitch at a time, making as small and even a stitch as possible.)

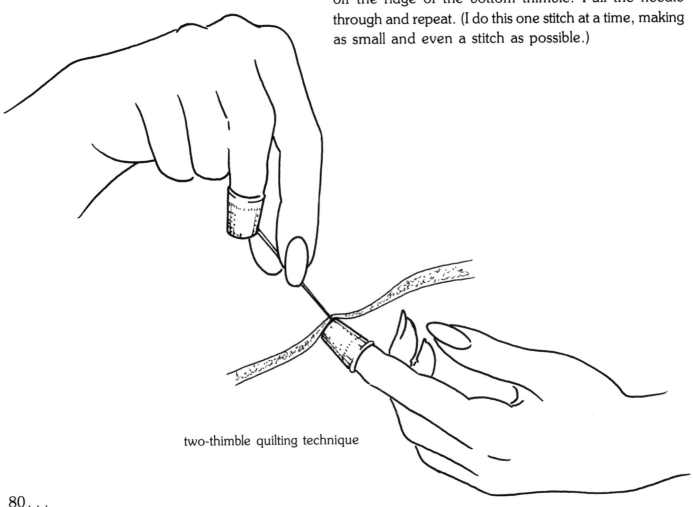

two-thimble quilting technique

.......BASTE, STRETCH, QUILT, AND BIND

When you get to the outside edge of the piece, and it will no longer fit into the hoop, baste a piece of muslin to the edge. Then, place your hoop on as before and continue quilting to the edge of the piece.

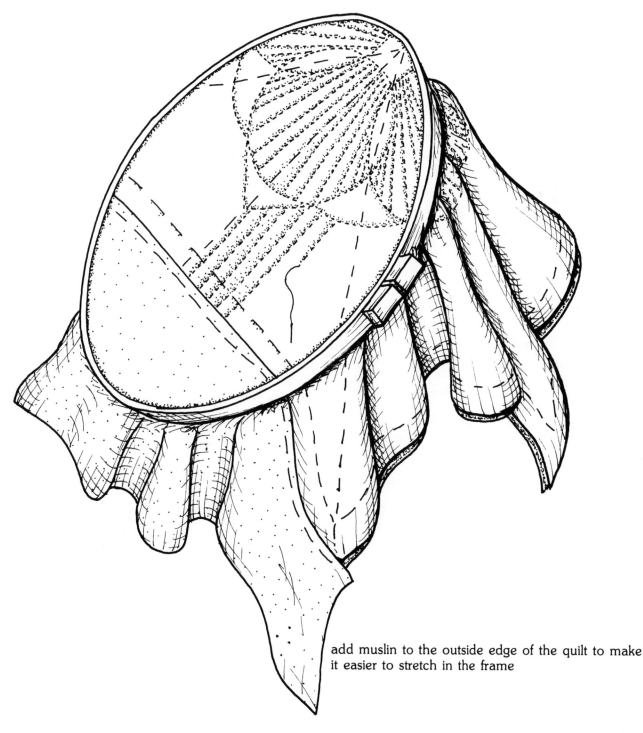

add muslin to the outside edge of the quilt to make it easier to stretch in the frame

BASTE, STRETCH, QUILT, AND BIND . . . .

BINDING . . . .

The last step is to bind the piece to finish it off. Trim the excess from the quilt.

Use the 49″ x 9″ piece of front fabric for the bias. Cut 1¾″ strips on the bias. (Bias is on the diagonal of the straight). Sew these strips together to form a strip long enough to go around the outside of the entire quilt. To do this, lay one strip of bias fabric face up, the next strip face down. The two pieces should overlap forming a 90° angle. The actual stitched line will be on the straight of the grain of both pieces. This stitched line will be a 45° angle to the inside edge of each piece. Trim away excess seam leaving only ⅛″. Press all of these seams open to form one straight long strip. Press in half lengthwise, wrong sides together.

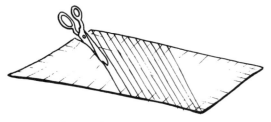

1) cut bias strips

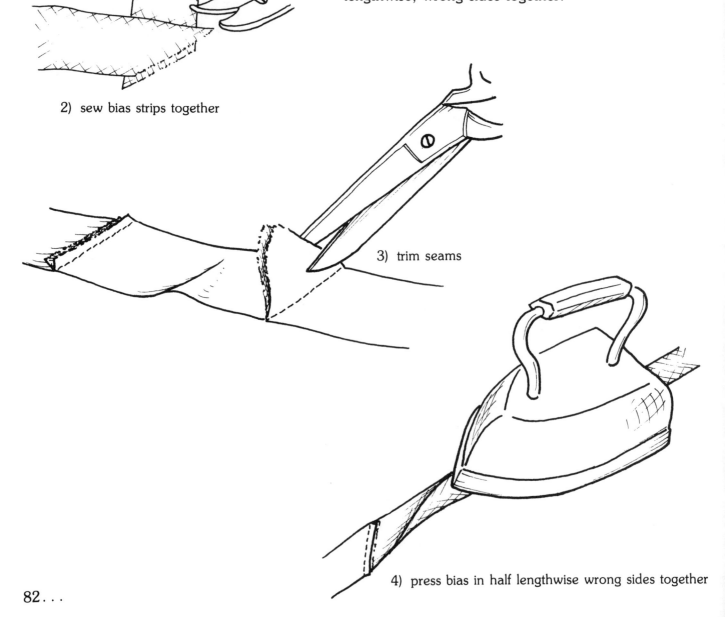

2) sew bias strips together

3) trim seams

4) press bias in half lengthwise wrong sides together

.......BASTE, STRETCH, QUILT, AND BIND

Sew the bias to the quilt with the raw edge of the bias matching the raw edge of the quilt. Machine stitch to front of the quilt. To begin sewing, fold one edge of bias over to create a finished edge. This folded edge should face up as you sew. Stitch with ¼″ seam, easing bias around corners and curves. Lap the end over the folded bias. Trim excess bias.

Trim seam to ⅛″ through all layers of backing, batting, top and binding. Roll folded edge of bias over trimmed seam to the back of the quilt and hand stitch in place.

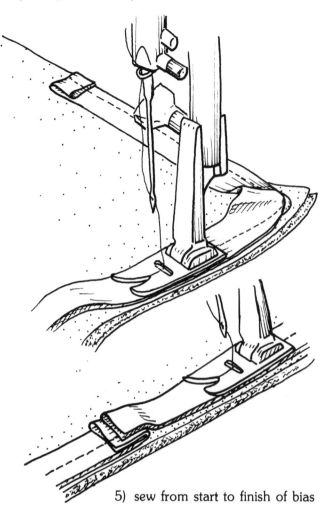

5) sew from start to finish of bias

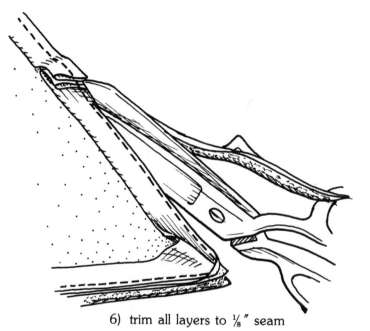

6) trim all layers to ⅛″ seam

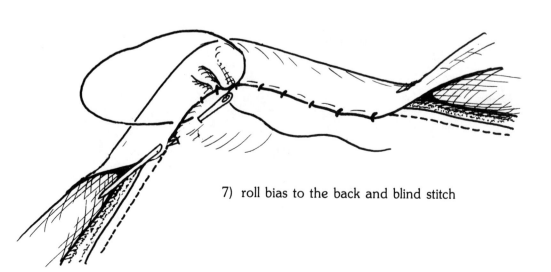

7) roll bias to the back and blind stitch

MANDALAS

Mandalas
        dia
            grams
    of uni
            verses
revolutions
        with centres
        without centres
within
without
without-within
                —John Douglas

                Mandalas

XII PIECING AND
CONSTRUCTION

PIECING AND CONSTRUCTION . . . .

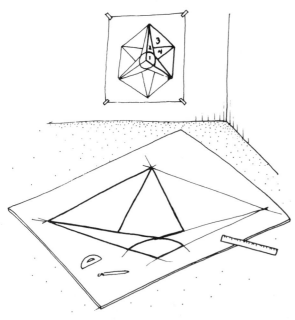

1) draft design onto template material

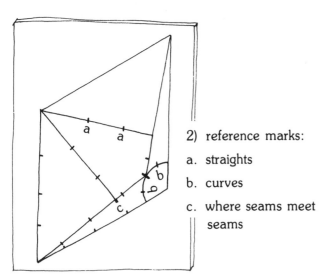

2) reference marks:
   a. straights
   b. curves
   c. where seams meet seams

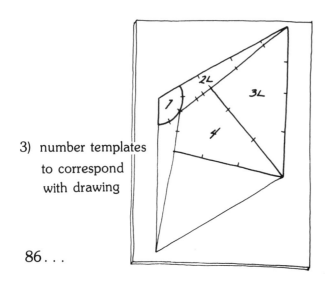

3) number templates to correspond with drawing

Up to this chapter we have been designing for a whole cloth mandala. Similar to drawing with fabric and thread, the paper becomes the cloth, and the pencil lines become the stitched lines. Now we will think about taking the mandala one step further by piecing it. The pencil lines will now become the pieced line.

The pieced mandala is created in the same manner as the whole-cloth mandala. Sometimes I design a whole-cloth mandala, then interpret that same design in a pieced mandala. (Plates 1a&b, 2a&b, 3a&b, 4a&b) This creates a set. My pieced mandalas are usually twice the size of the whole-cloth mandala.

Other times I design specifically for a pieced mandala and eliminate the whole-cloth. Whichever way you wish to work, the design process is the same. You still need to work with the basic divisions (chapter II). Play with lines and curves by any or all of the three methods: interlocking circles using a compass (chapter III), interlocking squares and shapes (chapter IV), or triangle units (chapter V).

Once you have a design you wish to piece, you need to enlarge it and make templates.

If you have done a whole-cloth mandala and wish to piece it, take this design and enlarge it. You can take the pattern for the whole-cloth and double the size using two as your ratio.

TEMPLATES . . . .

There are many different materials to make templates from — plastic, cardboard, X-ray film, etc. (I prefer to use a lightweight matte board and use an X-acto knife to cut it.) Draft one section of the design directly onto the template material. Follow directions on enlarging your design in chapter VIII. Be sure to check that the center angle is correct and the adjoining lines will match. Double check for accuracy, if you are off now, the whole quilt will be off.

Before the templates are cut it is very important to make reference marks. These will help the actual piecing be more accurate. (Reference marks are little lines that will be used to match seams, similar to notches used in dressmaking.) Make reference marks on straights, curves, and where seams meet other seams. Depending on the size of your templates, these marks should be roughly 4″ to 5″ apart.

.............PIECING AND CONSTRUCTION

Number the sections on one unit of your drawing that will be needed for templates. You only need one template for each shape. Some shapes will need to be reversed as you mark and cut the fabric. Cut out only the templates you need. Mark the templates with the corresponding numbers from the drawing. Put the templates together as you would a jigsaw puzzle on the corner of your cutting area. As you use a template, return it to its proper spot to avoid confusion.

If you have a piece that needs to be reversed for left or right side, label L or R and transfer markings to the back side. I do not add ¼ inch seam allowance to the templates. I mark the sewing line on my fabric, then cut by eyeballing ¼ inch seam allowances. (See next section, Marking)

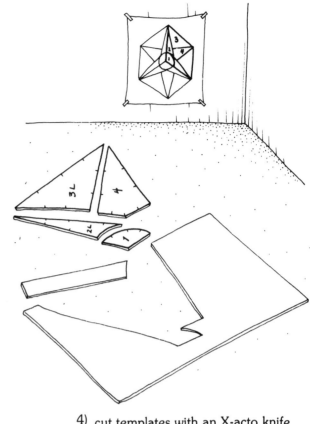

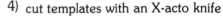

4) cut templates with an X-acto knife

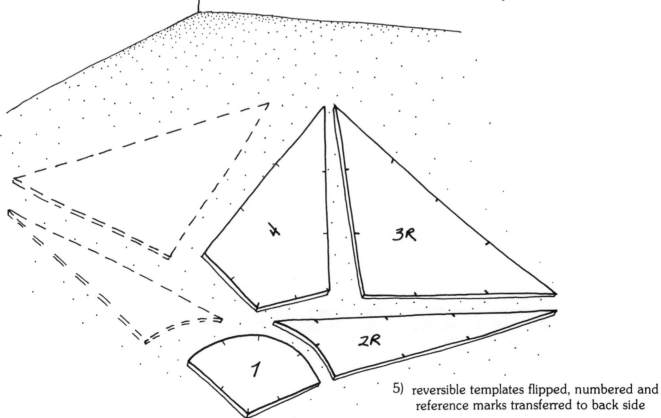

5) reversible templates flipped, numbered and reference marks transferred to back side

PIECING AND CONSTRUCTION . . . .

MARKING . . . .

Marking and color will be used simultaneously; read these two sections together before going any further.

Cut and mark your fabric one piece at a time. Press the fabric you are about to cut, then place the template upside down on the back or wrong side of the fabric. Mark around the template with a fabric marker. Transfer all reference points, then eyeball the ¼ inch seam and cut.

Pin fabric to the wall and continue. It is very easy to accidentally cut the reverse of the piece you want. If you have a template that is equal (can be cut either right side up or down), there will be no problem, but a lot of templates need to be reversed for left or right side. Hold the template up to the design on the wall in the direction it will need to be pinned up, then turn it upside down and place it on the wrong side of the fabric to mark.

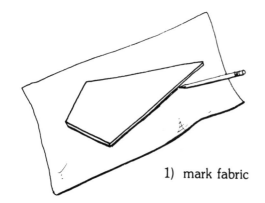

1) mark fabric

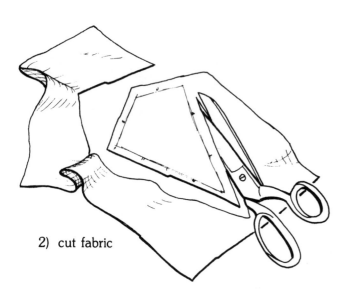

2) cut fabric

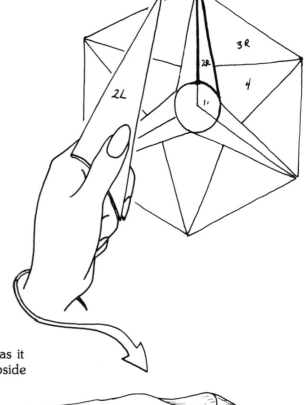

3) hold the template up to design on the wall as it should be pinned up then place template upside down onto the back of the fabric to mark

COLOR . . . .

Pin your design up on a wall, and sit back and study it. Decide where you want the color to go. (Read chapter XIV on color.) Lay the fabric out that you think you want to use. Do not be too stiff at this point; your color choices may change as you begin to pin them up and see how they interact with each other. Think of color runs, accents, different textures, and warm and cool colors. Each section may be identical, or you may wish to use different fabric and textures in each section. Cut each piece, then pin it to a wall. Felt or cork on a wall is an effective tool for pinning your pieces up in their proper place. In this way you are painting with cloth, and you can see your design develop in color before you. (I begin in the center, cut my fabric, pin up the pieces, then step back and view the piece through the wrong end of a pair of binoculars.)

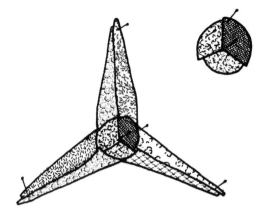

4) pin fabric to the wall working from the center out

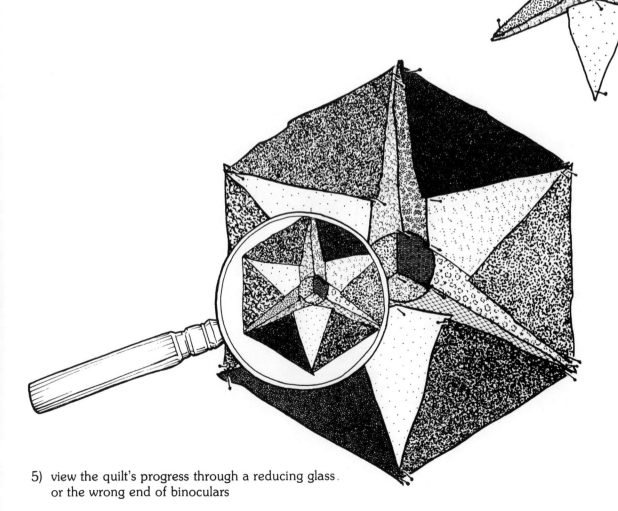

5) view the quilt's progress through a reducing glass. or the wrong end of binoculars

two possibilities of fabric placement

PIECING AND CONSTRUCTION . . . .

1) sew two triangles together

2) sew third triangle

3) add thin triangles

4) add center circle

5) sew triangle units together

ORDER OF SEWING . . . .

Do not panic once the whole-piece is pinned to the wall. Remember, we have been working in triangle units all through the book. Sewing will be done in the same manner. Working with just one unit, begin sewing smaller pieces together to form larger units. When one unit is pieced, move on to the other triangular units until they are all completed. Sew these units together to make the whole. Treat each of these seams as a straight seam. Pin the ends, and where seams need to match; sew and press open.

After the top is pieced and pressed, choose a complementary backing fabric and batting and baste the three layers together (see chapter X). Stretch in a hoop to quilt. Lastly, bind to complete this pieced mandala.

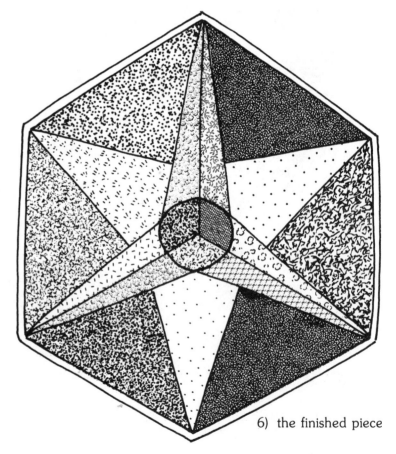

6) the finished piece

.............PIECING AND CONSTRUCTION

SEWING ....

Once the piece is all pinned to the wall and you are satisfied with the way everything looks, it is time to sew. There are three types of seams: straight seams, curved seams, and corners.

STRAIGHT SEAMS—When sewing two pieces of fabric together with straight seams, begin by pinning both ends, matching corners. Place a pin in each corner. Then pin to match reference marks. Depending on the length of the seam, pin in between as much as you need to feel comfortable. Pin through the lines to insure both seam lines will match.

Begin sewing at one end, starting right at the pin. Do one back stitch, then follow the marked line to the last pin, stop and back stitch. Press seams open.

Important: **Stop and start exactly at beginning and ending pins.**

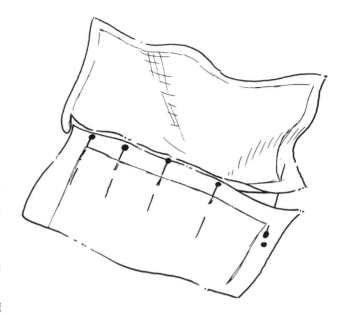

1) pin corners and notches

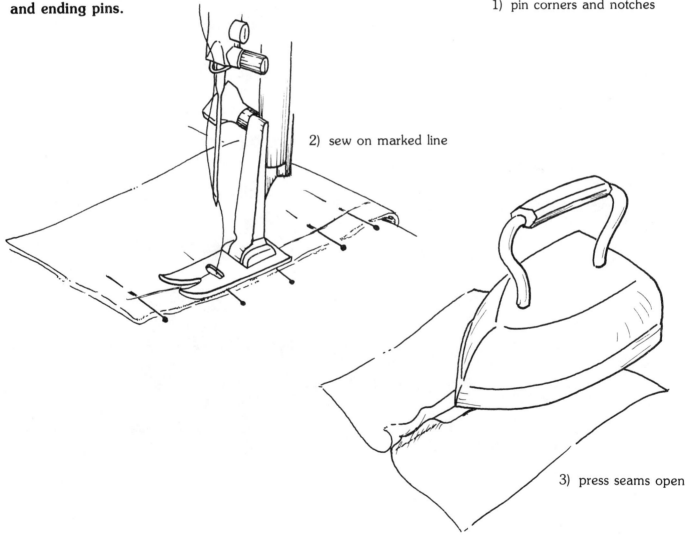

2) sew on marked line

3) press seams open

PIECING AND CONSTRUCTION . . . .

CURVED SEAMS — Pin the start and end of the seam. Continue pinning, matching reference points, ease if necessary. Pin in-between notches. The tighter the curve, the more pins that will be needed. Sew from start to finish, following the marked line. Sew with the inside curve on top. This piece will be ruffled. It will not lay flat.

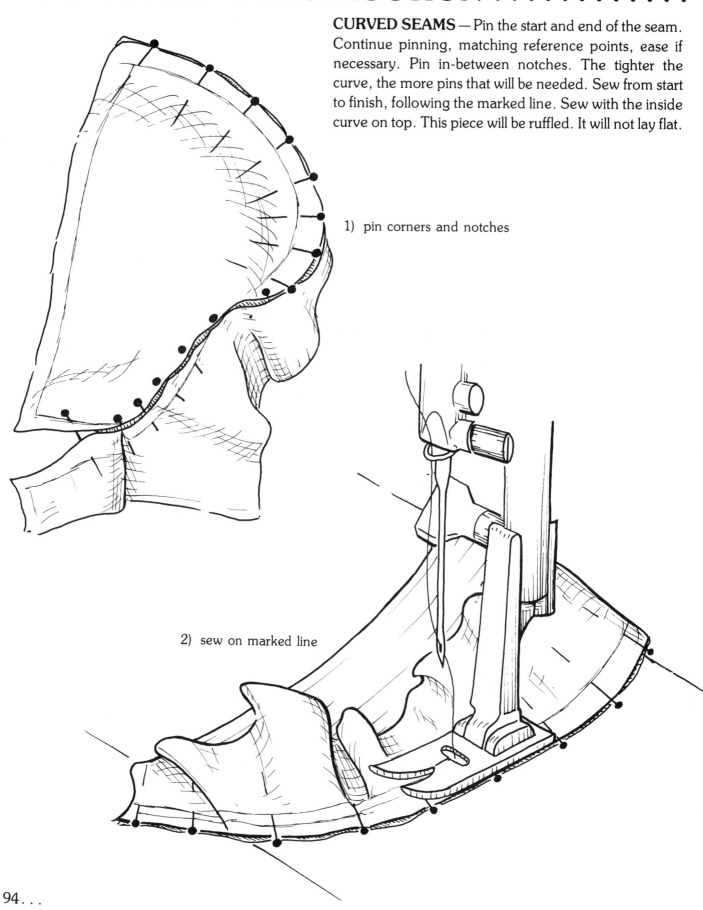

1) pin corners and notches

2) sew on marked line

...........PIECING AND CONSTRUCTION

CORNER SEAMS — Corners, as well as points, are treated as two separate straight seams. Pin corner to corner; match notches and sew *exactly* from one corner to the next. Clip the inside corner, stopping right where the seam ends. If this corner is not clipped, you will not be able to turn the fabric to pin the next seam.

Turn the fabric and pin corners and notches, and sew from exactly where the first seam ended in the corner to the other corner.

When you open it up, your corner should be exact. If not, check to see if you clipped in far enough, and that you have sewn exactly on the seam lines. All seams should be pressed open as they are sewn. Do not clip curves or seams, this weakens the seam.

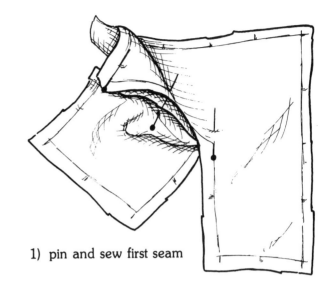

1) pin and sew first seam

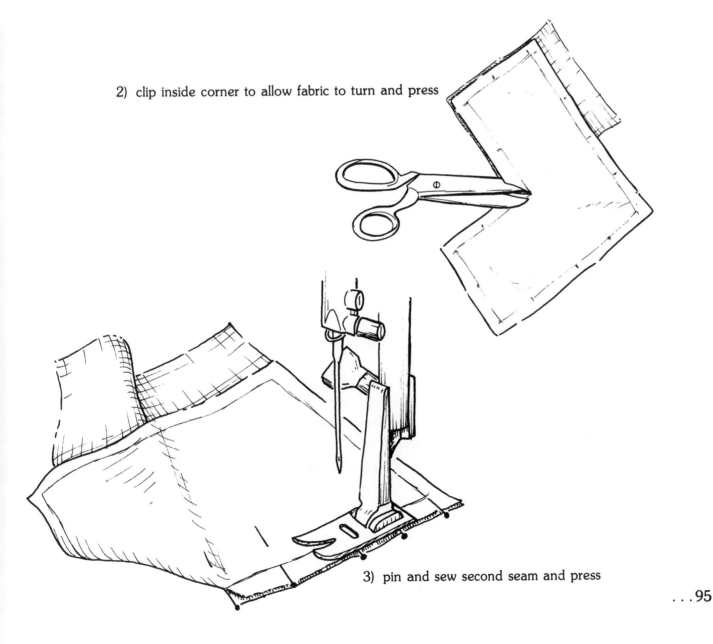

2) clip inside corner to allow fabric to turn and press

3) pin and sew second seam and press

You are led through your lifetime
by the inner learning creature,
the playful spiritual being that is your real self.
—Richard Bach

Illusions

XIII CREATIVE QUILTING

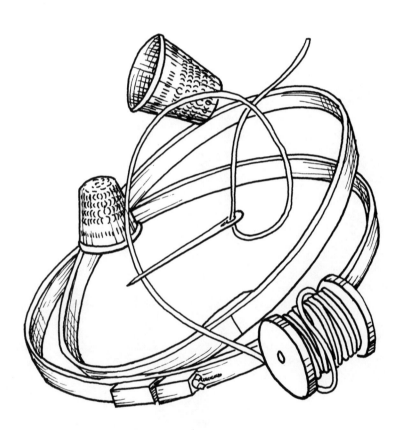

CREATIVE QUILTING ....

Whether you are quilting on a traditional pattern or an original mandala design, the quilting pattern should enhance the pieced design. Tradition has it that a quilt is stitched ¼ inch from each seam. Creative quilting breaks away from this mode, offering a greater choice for a quilting design. The actual quilting can be a totally different design from the pieced line. The two should merge to create a total picture.

To begin the creative quilting process, hang the quilt on the wall and study it. You may wish to refer to chapter VI on filler patterns to get ideas for quilting patterns. It is not necessary to figure out the quilting for the whole piece. Start by quilting the center sections, then rehang the quilt on the wall and determine the next step.

Section by section it will come together. The sections quilted will help determine how to quilt the next.

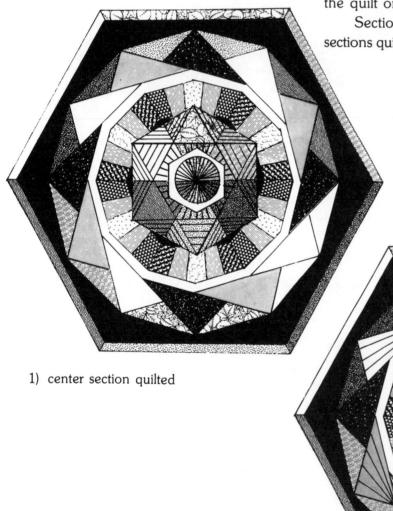

1) center section quilted

2) next section quilted

Quilting adds a new dimension to the pieced design. Quilting can make an otherwise flat piece come alive with action. As you can see from all of the color plates, the quilting pattern relates to the piece design, but is separate. Let the two lines, seam line and quilted line, interact with each other.

3) entire quilt quilted

CREATIVE QUILTING ....

In the quilt *Nova* (plate 1b), I chose to quilt a radiating pattern in the burgundy circles. On the navy-blue polished cotton, a basic grid was used. The border was quilted the opposite of the seam line. (The seam line curves one way, the quilted line curves in the opposite direction.)

Cosmic Kaleidoscope (plate 5) has a radiating pattern that envelopes the entire quilt.

Melanie's Rose (plate 9) is quilted with a variation of the grid, with lines going into the center to the vanishing point. It also has concentric circles on the yellow circles.

XIV COLOR

COLOR ....

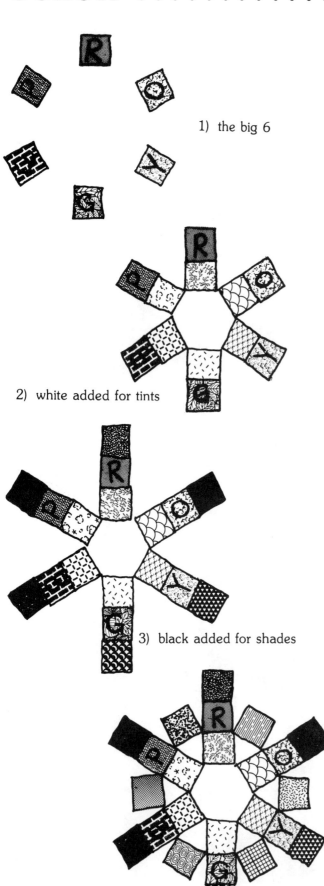

1) the big 6

2) white added for tints

3) black added for shades

4) blending colors

Col or (kul'er), n 1. the sensation produced by the different effects of waves of light striking the retina of the eye. **2.** the appearance of a thing, distinct from form, associated with the effect of particular vibrations of light coming from it; hue.

There are many wonderful books on color. I recommend some of these in the bibliography. It is a good idea to learn the proper principles of color. The type of color that I am going to address myself to is emotional color: the temperatures of color, how it speaks to you, primarily how the fiber artist deals with color through fabric.

COLOR WHEEL ....

It is important for all artists to have a color wheel made from the medium in which they work. *Color Wheel* (plate 8) and *CW II* (plate 14) are two examples of color wheels made from fabric.

To make a simple color wheel, you will need to go through your scraps to find the following colors. Primary colors: Red, Yellow, Blue; look for as pure and true a color as possible. Secondary colors: Orange, Green, Purple; prints as well as solids may be used in order to give more interest.

From now on, I will refer to these colors as the Big 6. To the Big 6 visually add white to create tints. To create shades, visually add black to the Big 6; then combine adjacent colors of the Big 6 to obtain the blending colors: Red-orange, Yellow-orange, Yellow-green, Turquoise, Violet, Burgundy. You will now have a basic color wheel. I have my students work with these colors in 2½″ squares. Several students took these rather simple color wheels and turned them into beautiful wall hangings. By adding borders and quilting, these become exciting mandalas in their own right. (See plates 15a thru 15k)

If you wish to design your own mandala color wheel, you will need to design it based on the division of 3 or 6 to have it work out right.

TEXTURE . . . .

Part of the excitement of working with fabric is the many types of textures available. Two basic types of texture are physical texture and visual texture. Physical texture is created by the cloth itself: satin has a smooth texture, while corduroy has a rough one. Visual texture is created by the colors on the cloth. This can be a solid color appearing smooth, or small and large prints appearing to be rough. Then there is always the combination of the two. Because of these textures, the variety of any one color is immense. If someone asked me to choose a black fabric from my scraps, I could come up with several possibilities: shiny black, dull black and printed blacks. The freedom of choice in choosing color for a quilt becomes doubly exciting.

As an example, if you have decided to use red for a section that repeats itself eight times in a mandala, why not use four different reds or six or all eight from different textures of reds. This makes the piece come alive.

TEXTURE STUDY — Go through your scraps and find as many different textures as possible of the same value of any one color. Cut these into equal size squares and pin them one right after another to the wall. Step back and view them through a reducing glass (or the wrong end of the binoculars); they should all look like the same color except for the different feeling they give because of their textures. The next time you need to use that color, use them all randomly in your quilt.

 satin

 corduroy

 cotton

solid color

small print

large print

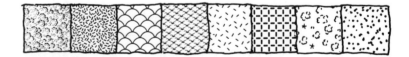

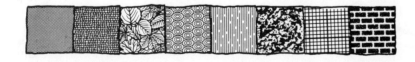

runs of textures of the same hue

COLOR . . . .

COLOR TEMPERATURES. . . . . . .

Colors all have a temperature to them, hot or cold, and varying degrees thereof. The hot colors are Red, Orange and Yellow. The cool colors are Green, Blue and Purple. Hot colors advance and appear larger; cool colors recede and appear smaller. This is due to the physical way in which the eye sees these colors. In *Color Perception In Art*, Faber Birren explains this phenomenon: Red normally focuses at a point behind the retina, causing the lens of the eye to become convex and to pull the red forward, making it appear both nearer and larger. Blue normally focuses at a point in front of the retina, causing the lens of the eye to flatten and to push the blue back making it appear farther away and smaller.

When working with your designs, decide which areas appear to be in the foreground; to make these areas stand out even more, use a warm color. Your eye will then physically pull that area towards you. Areas that you wish to appear behind should be done in cool colors. In the same sense, light colors come forward, while dark colors recede. Study the color plates to determine how warm and cool colors were used and how that choice enhanced the piece.

TEMPERATURE COLOR STUDY—Choose two colors of equal intensity, one warm and one cool, cut them into two squares of equal size. Pin them to a wall, stand back and see which one appears closer and larger and which one recedes and is smaller.

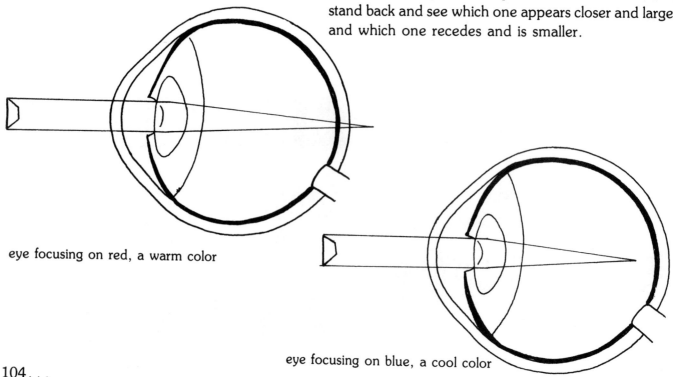

eye focusing on red, a warm color

eye focusing on blue, a cool color

LIGHT SOURCE . . . .

Often times adding a light source can change an ordinary quilt into one that is quite dynamic. In *Cosmic Kaleidoscope* (plate 5) the light source is in the very center of the quilt. First choose where the light source will be, then all of the colors near that source should be light. The colors should gradually become darker and darker as they get further and further from the light. In *Heavens Reach* (plate 2b), the light source is at the very top of the quilt, becoming darker as it reaches towards the bottom.

LIGHT SOURCE STUDY — These can also be called color runs. Start with white at the top and pure color in the middle, and black at the bottom. It is much easier to cut all your fabric into the same size squares to do these runs. Fill in the space gradually, blending towards black or white from the pure color. Once this is done, view the run through a reducing glass or binoculars. This is where the fabric begins to speak to you. If any one fabric does not belong, your eye will not flow smoothly from light to dark. The most common problem is using a dark background with white flowers or shapes printed on it. You will find these fabrics will not fit in on the dark side, because they appear too light, and they won't fit in on the light side, because they appear too dark. Eliminate them and look at the run again. Try this with several colors both cool and warm.

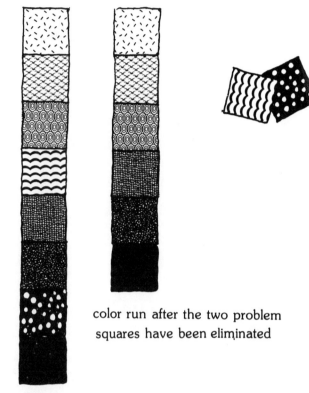

color run after the two problem squares have been eliminated

a color run with two fabrics that don't fit in

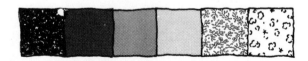

color runs from white to black

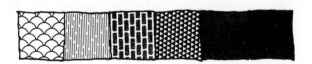

COLOR ....

1) color runs going in opposite directions

COLOR STUDY—As a final exercise to incorporate all that you have learned, make a color study. Take all of the fabric squares you have used so far and line them up into neat rows. Some things you may wish to think about are light source, textures, and how cool areas interact with warm. This will strictly be an emotional piece, there are no rules. The easiest way to begin is to lay the squares out in rows, continually viewing them through a reducing glass. As you work and view, things will begin to happen. Let the fabric guide you. Additional fabric should be added as needed. Relax and enjoy; everything will be right. There are no wrong solutions to this exercise. Each piece is individual.

   Some examples of student work can be seen in plates 15a thru 15k.

"Too much discipline runs the danger of discouraging the spirit rather than leaving it happily free. Science is essentially intellectual, art is essentially emotional."

– Faber Birren

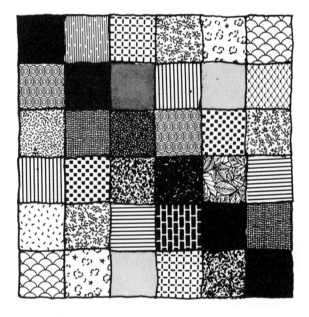

2) light source in opposite corners

3) light source in center

COLOR:

Birren, Faber, *Creative Color*. Van Nostrand
    Reinhold Company, 1961
Chevreul, M.E., *The Principles of Harmony and
    Contrast of Colors*. Van Nostrand Reinhold
    Company, 1967
Clark, Linda, *The Ancient Art of Color
    Therapy*. Pocket Books, 1975
Itten, Johannes, *The Art of Color*. Van
    Nostrand Reinhold Company, 1961

QUILTS:

Chase, Pattie, *The Contemporary Quilt*, E.P.
    Dutton, 1978
Fiberarts Magazine, *The Fiberarts Design Book*,
    Fiberarts, 1980
Gutcheon, Beth and Jeffrey, *The Quilt Design
    Workbook*, Rawson Associates Publishers,
    Inc., 1976
James, Michael, *The Quiltmaker's Handbook*,
    Leone Publications, 1993
James, Michael, *The Second Quiltmaker's Hand
    book*, Leone Publications, 1993

MANDALAS:

Arquelles, Jose and Miriam, *Mandala*,
    Shambhala 1972
Jung, Carl G., *Man and His Symbols*, Aldusbooks
    London ©1964
Jung, Carl G., *Mandala Symbolism*, Princeton
    University Press, 1959

Learning
is finding out
what you already know.
Doing is demonstrating that
you know it.
Teaching is reminding others
that they know just as well as you.
You are all learners,
doers, teachers.
—Richard Bach
Illusions